While We Wait

A Devotional for Those
Who Love the Prodigal

by Lynne Thompson

WHILE WE WAIT: A DEVOTIONAL FOR THOSE WHO LOVE THE PRODIGAL

Lynne Thompson

For permission requests, write to the authors at the address below: Pete & Lynne Thompson
8917 James Drive Lantana, TX 76226
PeteThompson.org

All Scripture quotations, unless otherwise indicated, are taken from the Holy Bible, New American Standard Bible (NASB) Copyright ©1960, 1962, 1963, 1968, 1971, 1972, 1973, 1975, 1977, 1995 by The Lockman Foundation, La Habra, CA. All rights reserved. Used by Permission.

ISBN: 979-8-218-65667-6

to those who wait

CONTENTS

INTRODUCTION

I never in a million years believed that I would be writing this book. Like many Christian families, I thought I'd followed all the rules. My husband and I are happily married and have done our best to live out biblical principles the best we knew how. We loved our children unconditionally and sacrificially. Our family life was homeschool and homemade cookies, Awana and Bible clubs, church and missions, silliness and laughter, sunny carefree summers and warm cocoon winters, discipline and direction, forgiveness and new beginnings. Both of my children would say their childhood was perfect. Yet, no one, and I mean no one, is immune from the pain of the prodigal. This is true of pastors, church leaders, authors, evangelists, counselors, couples that divorced, and couples that stayed together, those who homeschooled and those who did not. I stand shoulder to shoulder with many of those who left it all on the table, gave it all, and yet still...

Somewhere during our livin' the dream lifestyle, a child was lost. Not by death, although at times it feels like it, but in a dark forest of rebellion. At some point during the "growing up loved" and "learning to leave the nest" my child took the wide road; the one that led away from our family and all that we valued. I know I'm not alone. There are thousands of parents and family members just like me who are in shock, asking over and over again, "What happened?"

We can blame the culture, familial demons, that boy or girl that led them astray, or even ourselves, but at the end of the day the reasons fail to satisfy; we just want our child back, to return to the way things used to be before words were said and choices made that ripped apart the fabric of family. If you're like me you've spent a great deal of time, and an unbelievable amount of energy trying to come up with a solution, not to mention buckets of tears begging God to fix the broken. But eventually you come to the end of yourself and realize the truth...you cannot save the prodigal. Why? Because prodigals don't think they are lost. They love the world that tells them that it's okay to "live in sin" whether it's sexual, material, social, or religious. They believe the lie, they are deceived.

It was during this realization that I found peace; after all, it was no longer up to me. I am released from the responsibility of being my child's savior, truthfully, it was never mine to begin with. Realize that I said peace, not joy, at least not at first. There were many months now heading into years of trying to figure out my proper response to all of this. I could not participate in the sin, or provide comfort in rebellion, no, I wasn't called to be complicit. The other extreme is to pretend that those precious years loving my child never happened. Do I cut that person out of my heart? No, may it never be! I was chosen to be my child's parent for life, and this event did not catch God unaware. I have become acutely aware that stagnating in a sea of grief is not the answer. That is where our enemy resides, rubbing our noses in past mistakes, painting worst case scenarios, stealing our hope and joy, and sabotaging us from accomplishing prepared good works that glorify God. You may have heard it said that God's work is in the journey, and I'm determined to continue on His narrow road.

And that brings me to now, writing a new devotional for another season in life. And as I continue to pray for my prodigal's return, I have decided to faithfully walk this path that God has called me to traverse. I refuse to allow this time to be idle and fruitless. The last thing I want is to end up paralyzed in grief; that would be admitting defeat and trust me, I'm just getting started. As Paul writes in Romans 5:3-5, I will learn how to boast in my sufferings and rejoice in the hope of God's love.

So, please join me on this Holy Journey as we wait for our prodigals to come home.

I have sectioned off the devotional accordingly:

Truth Walk -A short truth taught from the Bible about the journey we are on, as we wait for our prodigal. Truth is important always, but especially during this crucial time when lies abound that run contrary to what God's word teaches. Psalms 145:18 tells us that the Lord is close to all that call on Him in truth. We definitely want the Lord to be near us during this time of trial, and it's the truth of God's word that helps us discern truth from lies.

Prayer-Words we call out to God as we seek His will for our prodigal and ourselves. James 5:16 tells us to confess our sins to each other and pray for each other so that we may be healed. Because it is the prayer of a righteous person that is powerful and effective.

Light- Bible verses that bring illumination to the things God wants us to meditate upon during this time. His word "is a lamp to my feet and a light to my path." We stand on the Word of God which is profitable, "**for teaching, for reproof, for correction, for training in righteousness; so that the man of God may be adequate, equipped for every good work.**" 2 Timothy 3:16.

Moving Forward- Sometimes concern or obsessing over the prodigal can cause us to become frozen or even fall back in our walk with God. These are things for you to do or meditate upon as you wait for your prodigal to come home. Ephesians 5:15-17 reads, "**Therefore be careful how you walk, not as unwise men but as wise, making the most of your time, because the days are evil. So then do not be foolish, but understand what the will of the Lord is.**"

Lastly, writing this book has been very difficult. I'm sure you understand. I want to be clear though, this journey is different for everyone. Praying through the many decisions and responses on how to respond to the prodigal requires "*hit the ground on your knees, crying out to God for wisdom*" kind of work. And perhaps this is exactly where our Lord wants us. Leaning into the Father with child-like trust and faith. So today we take a deep breath, and enter into a new adventure, trusting God fully with the ones that matter most.

--Lynne

❖   Please note that prodigals come in both sexes, son and daughter, granddaughter and grandson, niece and nephew, brother and sister, aunt and uncle. For writing clarity, and to acknowledge the prodigal as being either male or female I've chosen to address the prodigal in this book as She/He and Her/Him, so that all those who are waiting can identify with their individual prodigal.

DAY ONE - WHERE DID I GO WRONG?

Truth Walk

When a child does something horribly wrong it's typical for parents to ask themselves, "Where did we go wrong?" You relive memories where things could have perhaps contributed to a child's downfall, a time where discretion failed, or parental mistakes were made. You think back on how you could have done things differently if given the chance.

But the truth is, we are not perfect parents, because we are not perfect people. The Bible is clear that all have fallen short of the glory of God. Did you mess up sometime during your child rearing? Yes, of course you did, we all mess up somehow. God did not call us to be perfect parents. Why would he, knowing what he has to work with? We are painfully flawed. We could not raise a child perfectly no matter how hard we try because we cannot even conceive in our hearts what perfect is. Romans 3:10 tells us, "There is none righteous, not even one;" That's why Christ came; not so you could raise a child perfectly, but so that in your failure to parent perfectly, he would reconcile what is lost and fallen. If you parented perfectly, he wouldn't have needed to come. And parenting isn't all he needed to save. He came to save marriages, churches, families, the world, and you.

The other truth to realize is that your child isn't perfect either. Even when there were instances where you did things well, she/he can respond righteously or in sin. Your child gets to choose. You might help your child get a driver's license by investing time and money, making sure it's done properly to give him/her the best possible outcome. Your child then might choose his/her newfound freedom to drive to church events, work, school, or take food to the shut in, or he/she might use it to attend the latest drinking party or sneak around to attend something dangerous. So even if it was possible for your child to have the perfect parent, your child can still choose to sin.

As a former educator I never held to the old 'tabula rasa' theory which states that children are born innocent with a blank slate to write upon. Scripture tells us the opposite, in Psalm 51:5 we read, "Behold I was brought forth in iniquity, And in sin my mother conceived me." We are born in sin because mankind is fallen. Your child needs a Savior just as much as you do, and you are not it.

I remember months when I wallowed in the "where did I go wrong" mantra. My husband, a Christian therapist, exhausted from my rant one day said, "I will tell you the answer if you answer my question first." Finally, I praised, thinking I was going to get to the straight answer. He said, "God was a perfect Father, providing his children a perfect place, he gave them a perfect purpose, and perfect companionship, he supplied them with everything they would ever need without sin or sickness, so answer me, 'Where did He go wrong?" Needless to say, the answer is, "He didn't."

You see perfection isn't something we humans practice on this side of eternity. Our brain knows that it should exist, and at one time it did, but we chose death. So, in answer to the original question, "Where did I go wrong?" It happened in the garden; it happens every time I choose my own sinful desires over God's righteousness. To be honest, the next question is, "Where did I go right?" My answer is, "I told my child about a God who loves, and sent his Son to die for his/her sins, and mine."

Prayer

Dear Lord, thank you for saving me from my sin. Thank you that the same grace is extended to my child. Let the seeds of your truth that were planted in my child take root. Do not allow that enemy to snatch it away. Do not allow my child to fall away due to trouble or persecution. Do not allow the worries of life or the deceitfulness of wealth to choke out your words causing unfruitfulness. Let my child hear your word and understand it, causing a great and bountiful harvest in my child's soul. -Amen

Light

"The one who sins is the one who will die. The child will not share the guilt of the parent, nor will the parent share the guilt of the child. The righteousness of the righteous will be credited to them, and the wickedness of the wicked will be charged against them." Ezekiel 18:20

Moving Forward

Do not allow the enemy to blame you, he's good at that. He's a liar and talked Eve into a bad decision, and your child into a prodigal lifestyle. You live a righteous life not because of your great parenting, but because of Jesus. Start your day thanking God for his freedom from judgment because of the blood of Christ that covers your sin. We all rely on the same Savior; the same one your child will one day cry out to. Rejoice that with each day the clock ticks, the day Christ reconciles your child to himself draws closer.

DAY TWO - THE MAKING OF A TRUE BELIEVER

Truth Walk

We Christians have one hope for our prodigals that far surpass all other dreams. More than good health, a decent job, or finding a loving spouse, we want them to follow Jesus. We do many things to encourage this hope: take them to Sunday school, Awana, VBS, and various other church functions.

We try to live by example, nurturing our own walk with God. We pray, and pray, and pray. Still, there is one thing that must happen in order for our prodigal to develop the type of faith that surpasses a godly heritage…a prodigal must know God personally.

Sometimes I fret (a fancy way to say worry but the Bible says I shouldn't do that) when I look at where my prodigal is, and where I think my prodigal should be. Sometimes there are bad decisions made; painful ones that even God says are wrong. I have seen my prodigal question everything that I so diligently taught over the years. Did I miss a step? Yes, God assured me I had, it was the one where I forgot to step back and let Him work in my prodigal's life.

If I'm truly honest about my own faith walk, I have to confess that my greatest commitments came about during the toughest times in my life, time spent with me and God wrestling it out Jacob style. My faith is authentic, not inherited from someone else, and last I checked there is no God chromosome. A relationship with God isn't like a well-intended hand-me-down; God is not in the second-hand store business.

What I want for my prodigal is an honest faith that will carry my prodigal through this lifetime and onto the next. My prodigal is on a journey to the cross and journeys usually take more than a day, sometimes years. The scriptures are clear about God's intentions, "Come now, and let us reason together, 'Says the Lord, "Though your sins are as scarlet, They will be as white as snow; Though they are red like crimson, They will be like wool." You see God isn't in denial about the sin, he is basically saying, "you have red stained sin all over you and I see it, but I'm offering you a solution to clean you up and make everything brand new like white snow and bleached wool."

But he makes it clear, "they will be" identifies the current condition and the change that will come when a person is ready, but only after they have "reasoned" or come to their senses with God. The word "reason" in Isaiah 1:18 is the word we use in legal cases. We reason or judge if someone is to be punished or vindicated and cleared of blame for their sins. However, God is ready to acquit, not because the red stained sin is nonexistent, but because the prodigal is pronounced "not guilty" by a loving God who takes the sin upon himself and pays the price.

Unfortunately, we can't make someone come to their senses. Only God can do that. John 6:44 says it this way, "No one can come to Me unless the Father who sent Me draws him; and I will raise him up on the last day." Knowing this truth encourages us as we wait for the Father to do his best work, drawing the prodigal in, causing the prodigal to come to his/her senses, acquitting the prodigal of all sin, cleansing the prodigal, and rising the prodigal up on the last day. I know I wouldn't want to borrow anyone else's faith in God; it would not have been enough to get me through the tough times I've already had to survive. Therefore, it would be absurd for me to expect my prodigal to borrow my faith for his/her life. Authentic faith is the goal. Fortunately, we serve a good God who can make that happen.

Prayer

Dear Lord,

Thank you for drawing me into a deep relationship with you. Help me to remember how you used situations in my life to bring me to your salvation. Help me to step back and watch the Master save my prodigal. Thank you that your desire is that none should perish, including my precious prodigal. -Amen

Light

"For the Son of Man came to seek and to save the lost." Luke 19:10

Moving Forward

Write a salvation thank you letter to God. Include some of the circumstances that led you to cry out to God and receive Him as Lord and Savior of your life.

DAY THREE - GOD WORKING IN THE SILENCE

Truth Walk

I'm at teller. Not the kind you find at the bank, but the kind you find offering my wanted (or unwanted) opinion on what you should be doing or not doing. You can't blame parents for their propensity to be bossy in their prodigal's life. When you raise a human being and have definitive evidence where, on more than one occasion, you have saved them from harm, bad decisions, or even death, you believe you have merited respect and the right to be heard.

This kind of track record might prove beneficial to someone with wisdom. The Bible speaks of this in Proverbs 13:1, "A wise son accepts his father's discipline, but a scoffer does not listen to rebuke" and in Proverbs 13:14, "The teaching of the wise is a fountain of life, to turn aside from the snares of death." No, the problem here isn't your previous accolades. Most likely your prodigal remembers your loving and many times divinely led interventions, but to him/her it no longer matters, because at this time in his/her life, he/she is a scoffer and wisdom escapes him/her.

To be wise three things must happen:

- Know that you are not practicing wisdom

   (Proverbs 3:7)
- Fear God (Proverbs 9:10)
- Turn away from evil (Proverbs 4:27)

When any, or all, of these three are absent from a person's life there is no wisdom. And when you give advice to the unwise or someone practicing foolishness it doesn't go well. The term scoffer is defined as "someone who laughs and speaks about a person or idea in a way that shows that they think that person or idea is stupid or silly." Here is the biblical warning about trying to talk sense into a scoffer in Proverbs 9:7-8 "He who corrects a scoffer gets dishonor for himself, And he who reproves a wicked man gets insults for himself. Do not reprove a scoffer, or he will hate you, Reprove a wise man and he will love you."

When I read this passage, I am reminded of how many times dishonor follows reproving a prodigal. The age old saying of "spitting into the wind" comes to mind. But this is not how God wins over the prodigal. He doesn't bother correcting the scoffer; he allows bad decisions do that. In Galatians 6:7-8 we read, "Do not be deceived, God is not mocked; for whatever a man sows, this he will also reap. For the one who sows to his own flesh will from the flesh reap corruption, but the one who sows to the Spirit will from the Spirit reap eternal life."

God has set up a world that is full of consequences, and just like us, he wants his children to avoid all the decisions that lead to bad ones. The Bible is full of these warnings, which aren't so much a list of do nots, but rather a list of how to avoid pain and trouble. But when we don't listen to God he doesn't need to give us lectures (something my children say I'm very good at), no, he lets the consequences speak for themselves. And eventually they do... every time.

Let's be honest, you've spent your entire life speaking life into your prodigal, and now she/he wants none of it. Your prodigal already knows what you think; already knows what you will say. She/He has become a good Jedi student and studied you well, but at this time doesn't want to hear the voice of truth.

Let God do the talking through the reaping and sowing of the prodigal's decisions. When the time is right, your prodigal will be ready to listen. Not with, "I told you so," but with, "I know, I've experienced it too."

Prayer

Dear Lord, Please let me be silent while you work in my prodigal's life. Let the seeds of your word planted into my prodigal rise up at your appointed time. I know that your word is powerful and does not return void, and is sharper than a two edged sword. I choose to trust your word in my own life. Make me wise Lord. Help me practice wisdom, fear God and have reverence for your will. Let me turn from evil and follow your plan. Amen

Light

"The Lord will fight for you while you keep silent." Exodus 14:14

Moving Forward

Write what you want to tell your child in a note, seal it and don't send. Take it to your prayer closet and offer it up to God. Trust him to act in your child's best interests.

DAY FOUR - SEPARATION

Truth Walk

I used to joke with my husband that it would be less painful for my arm to be severed from my body than to lose one of my children. I viewed being separated from my child akin to losing a part of my own flesh. In a way it's true. My prodigal and I were inseparable. We laughed, we shopped, we designed, we dreamed, we ate out and laughed some more. But separation hasn't always been bad, for me or my prodigal. I needed some perspective. I needed time to find out who I am without my child, and likewise my child needed to become familiar with who she/he is apart from me.

Time is an interesting thing. It makes things clearer by looking at previous situations with less emotion but greater insight. I wonder if that's how Joseph (the coat of many colors guy, Genesis 37) felt. I'm sure after his brothers sold him into slavery first and foremost on his mind were ways to murder each of them when given the chance. Then came a false accusation and prison. He must have been very angry. If his brothers hadn't acted wickedly, he'd be home getting another new coat. But then Joseph had time to think while in prison, about ten years according to most biblical scholars.

I can't even fathom being apart from my prodigal for ten years, but ten years is what it took to change Joseph's heart from seeking revenge to accepting God's plan. Not that he didn't toy with the idea of revenge. When his brothers arrived in Egypt looking for food during a famine, they didn't recognize him. Joseph then set them up to look like robbers. As the second most powerful man in Egypt he could have had them killed, no questions asked. But he didn't.

Time had done its work on his soul, and his sorrows of days past had matured into insight for a much bigger plan. We read where his heart landed in Genesis 50:20, "As for you, you meant evil against me, but God meant it for good in order to bring about this present result, to preserve many people alive." Joseph knew that if things had gone his way many people would have died and his people would have vanished from the earth. He knew that God had called him apart for something bigger, something revenge would have destroyed.

Time does something that nothing else can; it corners us with our circumstances and causes us to look outside ourselves at other possibilities. You start to understand that maybe life is not about you. Maybe God has bigger or different plans. I'm no prophet by any means, but I'm expectant that the same God who turned Joseph, a spoiled, self-absorbed rich kid, into a humble, forgiving, and wise leader, can, through time, reach my child and bring about His great plans for his/her life.

I'm even more hopeful that the plans I had dreamed of for myself have been changed for a reason, and that my plan pales in comparison to what God has in store. I don't know what circumstances it will take for me and my prodigal's heart to change into the person God can use for his glory, for his purposes that reach beyond my current situation. I'm looking forward to the good outcome; you could say I'm counting the days, however many God deems necessary.

Prayer

Dear Lord, Use this time in my prodigals life to mold him/her into the leader you need for this time in history. Also use this time in my life to root out the things that you cannot use and replace them with fruits that further your kingdom. Do not let me waste another day fretting, but rather grateful that time is in your hands, to be used your way, for your kingdom. Amen

Light

"He has made everything beautiful in its time. He has also set eternity in the human heart; yet no one can fathom what God has done from beginning to end." Ecclesiastes 3:11

Moving Forward

Don't waste this time. God is preparing you just as much as he's preparing your prodigal for kingdom work. Ask God what your "next" is. Sign up for a Bible class, take up an instrument, start a ministry.

DAY FIVE - A PEEK INTO THE FUTURE

Truth Walk

Some of you may remember the old I Dream of Jeannie television series from the 60's. One day I found myself watching an episode where Major Nelson was being transferred to another job far away, which of course brought sorrow to both Jeannie and, his buddy, Major Healey. So together, they concocted a plan to let Major Nelson peer into a movie machine that showed the future, hoping that this would help him see the pitfalls of accepting this new position and change his mind. Unfortunately for them, the future looked pretty promising; the job had many perks, including gorgeous secretaries at Major Nelson's disposal. Of course that would never do! So Jeannie drummed up some of her magic and showed him a false future, one filled with unbelievable trials, and disasters. It was a peer into the future, but none of it was true.

As I sat watching the show I couldn't help but wonder about my visions of the future, and question who was controlling my movie machine. What we see now is but a slice in time, and when we try to deduce what the future will look like, it can be pretty terrifying, especially when Satan is running the projector. The last thing our enemy wants is for us to have hope. If we have hope, than Satan's power to manipulate and control us decreases. Instead, we are to allow God to guide us in his truth and teach us, why? "...For you are God my Savior, and my hope is in you all day long." (Psalms 25:5 NIV). When we rest on an all-powerful God, the serpent is rendered ineffective in our lives and in our minds.

God's word has an opinion regarding our feeble attempts at future peering. It was Jesus who said, "So do not worry about tomorrow; for tomorrow will care for itself. Each day has enough trouble of its own." (Matthew 6:34) We are instead asked to rest on the promises that God has for my future. In Jeremiah 29:11 we read, For I know the plans that I have for you,' declares the Lord, 'plans for welfare and not for calamity to give you a future and a hope."

There are many times throughout the day when my mind starts to gaze ahead and daydream upon possible realities regarding my prodigal that haven't even transpired. They scare me, and they cause me to question a good and loving God. After all, no one could have predicted the benefits of tossing Joseph in prison, forcing Esther into a dangerous decision, or hemming in an entire nation of escaping Hebrews up against a sea. It's in those "didn't see that coming" moments that trust is essential for our survival. So I've made a pact with myself to ignore the lies of the future machine, and instead microwave some popcorn and watch what God can do.

Prayer

Dear Lord, let me fix my gaze upon you the finisher and perfector of our faith. Jesus please clear my mind of dark thoughts, and replace them with your truth. Teach me trust in your ways that are far above anything I could ever imagine. Amen

Light

(Regarding Satan) "He was a murderer from the beginning, and does not stand in the truth because there is no truth in him. Whenever he speaks a lie, he speaks from his own nature, for he is a liar and the father of lies." John 8:44b.

Moving Forward

When you are tempted to peer into the "crystal ball" of life, write a list starting with Genesis and record the catastrophic possibility of what could have happened, and then write what happened instead. God's track record of intervening in the affairs of man is quite impressive indeed. Here are a few to get you started:

Genesis 7
Could have happened: Noah and his righteous family drowned in the flood
What happened Instead: God flooded the entire earth and saved Noah and his family

Genesis 50
Could have happened   All of Egypt and Israel starved
What happened Instead: Rescued Joseph from prison, made him a leader, saved many nations.

Exodus 12
Could have happened   Killed all of the first born in Egypt.
What happened Instead: Passed over the Hebrews who marked the doors with blood.

Judges 7

Could have happened	Gideon defeated by the Midianites due to a small army.
What happened Instead:	God further scaled down Gideon's army and defeated the enemy.

John 8

Could have happened:	Condemned and stoned the woman for adultery.
What happened Instead:	Brought conviction upon the accusers and sent them away.

Matthew 28

Could have happened:	Mankind is judged and sentenced to eternal damnation.
What happened Instead:	God's love sent Christ to die for man's sins, rise on the third day, and gather his own to eternal life.

DAY SIX - THE RESPONSE TO JUDAS

Truth Walk

Jesus had a prodigal disciple; his name was Judas Iscariot. After following Jesus for most of his three-year ministry, Judas decided to betray Jesus by turning him over to the authorities for death, for the price of 30 pieces of silver. This did not come as a surprise to Jesus. Judas, the son of perdition was prophesied by the prophet Zechariah, and then Judas met a tragic end. Of course, we all pray for a good outcome for our own prodigals and cannot even imagine a similar fate. Still, we can learn a lot about how Jesus dealt with Judas. Here are a few lessons to be learned.

Lesson One: Trust in the Divine Plan

Judas' betrayal did not in any way tarnish the reputation of what Jesus had accomplished. We get a hint about this by reading about Jesus' prayer to the Father in John 17:12," While I was with them, I was keeping them in Your name which You have given Me; and I guarded them and not one of them perished but the son of perdition, so that the Scripture would be fulfilled." Here we see that Jesus wasn't focused upon the decision of Judas, but rather the obedience to the call of his Father. There was no mistake, the prophecy was fulfilled with Judas' decision. Jesus, under the power of God's will, submitted to the situation, he bowed to his Father's decision to carry out events as ordained.

Lesson Two: Do the Lord's work regardless of the outcome

Based upon the earlier prayer prayed by Jesus, he knew the outcome of Judas, yet you don't see a moment where Jesus treated Judas differently than the other disciples. Judas had a front row seat to all of Jesus' teachings. He was given the responsibility as treasurer for the group. He stayed in the same camp. He was sent out two by two to preach and given the ability to heal. He knew of Jesus itinerary (which is how he betrayed Jesus). He had his feet washed the same as the others and participated in the Lord's Supper. Still, Jesus didn't show favoritism in an effort to win Judas over, nor treat him less in anticipation of his betrayal. Jesus gave Judas every opportunity to repent, to obey.

Lesson: Do not pretend that sin is acceptable

When it came to exposing sin, Jesus wasn't shy. We remember him calling out the Pharisees as blind guides, whitewashed tombs, and brood of vipers destined for hell. He was no different with Judas. Calling out Judas's sin In Matthew 26:24 he said, "The Son of Man is to go, just as it is written of Him; but woe to that man by whom the Son of Man is betrayed! It would have been good for that man if he had not been born." Sin is serious business, and pretending there is no sin, where sin is brazen, is deceitful. Being complicit by hiding the reality of the sin, instead of bringing it out into the open, means that the lost remain hidden in their sins.

Lesson: Accept the suffering with which God has entrusted to you

We are called in the book of James to count it all joy when we face trials, those difficult events produce in us things that are good: perseverance, maturity, and completeness. But for Jesus the suffering was his calling. We read in Isaiah 53, "He was despised and rejected by mankind, a man of suffering, and familiar with pain. Like one from whom people hide their faces he was despised, and we held him in low esteem." How did Jesus handle the call to a betrayal by one of his own? As the guards approached to apprehend Jesus, he did not rebuff Judas' kiss. Jesus didn't fight back. In fact, when Peter attempted to fight back by striking the high priest's servant, and taking off his ear, Jesus responded by healing the man, and then rebuffed violence as recorded in John 18:11, "So Jesus said to Peter, "Put the sword into the sheath; the cup which the Father has given Me, shall I not drink it?" Receiving the suffering that God has chosen for us is difficult, but Jesus chose to demonstrate the proper response that obedience often requires.

Prayer

Dear Lord, there are times when I feel the same emotions and frustrations you must have felt while here on earth. Betrayal is a tough one. Yet, you trusted the Father with his divine plan. You called out the darkness that kept people enslaved in sin. You stood strong in your suffering, knowing that God has a plan. You loved unconditionally, even to those who made it difficult. Please help me imitate you and how you responded to hard things. I will trust you with this season in my life. I will acknowledge the goodness of God. Amen

Light

"Behold, My servant will prosper, He will be high and lifted up and greatly exalted." Isaiah 52:13

Moving Forward

Write your list of current sufferings, then hand them over to God in prayer. Thank God for these and claim the outcome by writing them down where you can regularly see them.

- I will have perseverance
- I will have maturity
- I will be complete, lacking nothing

DAY SEVEN - TRUST AND OBEY

Truth Walk

Let's be honest for a minute. Prodigals who walk away from God do bad things. Not all prodigals are the same and they do different kinds of bad things, some lie, cheat, steal, some commit crimes, some engage in sexual depravity, some replace God with idols be it money, fame, or relationships. What all prodigals have in common is they have run away from the word of God, and continually walk in ways that are antithetical to the gospel; that is what makes them prodigals. This defiance does more than hurt the relationship between the prodigal and God, it breaks the trust between us and them.

The behavior of the prodigal ushers in many feelings that are difficult to process. In many ways the emotions mirror those who go through the 5 stages when losing a loved one to death.

Denial　　　"Did this really happen? How could I have missed this?"

Anger　　　"How ungrateful is my prodigal and how mean is God who allowed this to happen after I raised a Christian child?"

Bargaining　　"What do I need to do Lord to fix this?"

Depression　　"This is hopeless I've lost my child, my life is too difficult to move forward in ministry."

Acceptance   "This is my new calling, even though I don't understand. Yet, I will trust in my sovereign God.

These feelings are normal. Of course, the difference between a death and a living prodigal is the anticipated hope that someday things will be different. But if we are honest, we can admit that although things might be different, they will never be the same. Trust broken is very hard to regain. There is always that empty feeling that one will be hurt again, it's a risk for sure. In the Bible we are often asked to do things that are hard. It is never easy to walk by faith and not by sight. It is never easy to deny ourselves and take up our cross and follow Jesus no matter what. It is never easy to endure various trials. Yet we are commanded to do all the above, using Christ's strength to accomplish them. It should not be surprising that the Apostle Paul once asked someone he knew to do something very difficult.

In one of Paul's letters in the Bible we are introduced to the difficult book, Philemon. Its difficulty lies in the issue surrounding slavery. It is important to understand that slavery was not always practiced the way we understand slavery today. Many voluntarily sold themselves or were sold in order to pay back debt, the alternative being debtor's prison (see Matthew 18:23, 30).

In this book of the Bible, Philemon, a debt slave owner and leader of the church of Colosse, (who also received the letter from Paul to the Colossians), is asked by Paul to forgive his former debt slave Onesimus. The debt slave had committed two crimes that we are aware of against his master. First, he ran away without paying off his debt, and secondly, he robbed Philemon of money, both punishable under Roman law. While in prison Paul met Onesimus and shared with him the gospel message. Onesimus repented and became a Christian. And although Onesimus was a great blessing to Paul while he was in prison for preaching the gospel, Paul sent his newfound convert back home to his master. The letter is Paul's request to Philemon to accept him back as a brother in Christ.

This was most likely a difficult letter for Philemon to receive. He had to again trust someone who had betrayed him in the past.

Had he really changed? Would he rob Philemon again? It was Paul who reminded Philemon of truths that we need to consider when we are asked to welcome back a prodigal into our lives:

There is repentance - In verse 16, we read the words, "a beloved brother" and "in the flesh and in the Lord." The slave was not the same person he used to be, his newfound relationship with God had transformed him.

His debt would be paid - In verse18, Paul promises to pay back the debt of any damage that the slave had inflicted upon his master. At the same time, however, Paul reminds Philemon that he too owes a debt that he cannot pay; Paul had shared with Philemon the gospel that brought forth a transformed life and freedom from sin.

God is sovereign over the circumstances - in verse 15, we see Paul embracing the same concept in Genesis 50:20, when Joseph said, "As for you, you meant evil against me, but God meant it for good in order to bring about this present result, to preserve many people alive." Paul is reminding Philemon that sometimes God allows less than desirable circumstances according to our estimation, in order to accomplish the will of God.

In the end, Philemon did not have a slave, but a brother and partner in ministry, no different than the partnership shared between Philemon and the apostle Paul. Trust is a difficult thing, and betrayal hurts, yet God is asking us to embrace the repentant prodigal, and how can we not when we ourselves accept the embrace of a forgiving God.

Prayer

Dear Lord, as we prepare for the prodigal return remind us of our own need for repentance. Thank you for using this time that might seem wasteful to us, but in reality, will be used for good in the hands of a loving and all powerful God. Amen

Light

"And we know that God causes all things to work together for good to those who love God, to those who are called according to His purpose." Romans 8:28

Moving Forward

Write a list of things that you thought were bad things in your life that God turned around and used it for your benefit and his purpose.

DAY EIGHT - HOW WE PRAY

Truth Walk

I've always prayed for my children, even before they were born. I've kneeled beside their bed and prayed for their salvation, for wisdom, for protection. But there have been times when my prayers have puzzled my children. I remember such a time when my son was in grammar school, and he came home upset with a detention slip in his hand. I asked what he had done to deserve this punishment.

"It's not fair!" he bemoaned, "we were having a staple gun fight in class and I was the only one who got caught." I told him it was most likely because I prayed. "You prayed that I would get into trouble?" he questioned. I explained it was just the opposite. "I always pray that your sins would be found out so that you don't think sin is a good idea. That way you stay far away from permanent troubles," I said.

"What kind of Mom prays like that!" he shouted. "One who loves you," I assured. When it comes to the prodigal it's sometimes hard to know how to pray. But if you are someone who loves a prodigal, and wants your prodigal back walking with God, you might have to pray some really hard prayers. Ones that make us look cruel on the outside, but desperately praying for repentance and reconciliation on the inside.

How we pray for our prodigal is important, not just for him/

her but for our own relationship with God. One of my favorite passages in scripture that makes me giggle every time is found in Joshua 5:13-15. The children of Israel are preparing themselves to take the city of Jerico in the Promised Land, when a man shows up sword in hand. Joshua asks the stranger, "Are you for us or for our enemies?" The man answers, "Neither, but as commander of the army of the Lord I have now come." It didn't take Joshua long to realize he wasn't dealing with just anyone, he was speaking to God in human form. Joshua quickly assessed that it was he who needed to pick the right side, not the other way around.

The funny part is that Joshua wanted to make sure God was on his side, not his enemy's side, but God is always on his own side. We think we know how to pray for the prodigal, and we want God to be on the side of our ask, but if we aren't careful to submit to God and his methods, we might be working against God's plans for success.

Let's remember the story Jesus told of the prodigal in Luke 15. The story begins with a son who was foolish and rebellious after demanding, and then receiving, his family inheritance. The prodigal went on to squander the money on loose living, eventually leading to poverty and hunger. Meanwhile, his father back home could have prayed, "Please give my son lots of success and never allow him to go hungry." But that prayer falls short, since it was the financial failure and the hunger that drove the prodigal to repent and return home.

The apostle Paul understood this principle well. When confronting the Corinthian church in 1 Corinthians, chapter 5. Paul rebuked the church members who were harboring the sinful behavior of other believers, in an attempt to show how tolerant they were. Paul's solution was to "deliver such a one to Satan for the destruction of his flesh, so that his spirit may be saved in the day of the Lord Jesus." 1 Corinthians 5:5. Paul understood that painful consequences are many times the catalyst for change.

Unfortunately, we humans often lack the necessary patience it takes to see it through when God is working on the heart of a person. The process can be pretty messy. John 6:44 says, "No one can come to Me unless the Father who sent Me draws him; and I will raise him up on the last day." The word, *draw* in Greek (*helkuo*) means to drag. This means that God is in the business of taking the unwilling (that's all of us) and supernaturally dragging the sinner to a place of repentance. He does this dragging with the end goal in mind, "Raise him up on the last day." We aren't even able to come to the Father without his insistent love, pursuing us until the end.

I'm not going to tell anyone how to pray for their prodigal, but I will encourage you to first seek the perspective of God who wants to save the soul and might need to use suffering, time, and consequences to achieve that goal. Join God in his quest as he pursues his lost sheep using his methods. He knows what will drive him/her back into the fold.

Prayer

Dear Lord, your ways are not my ways, and your thoughts are higher than mine. You know my precious prodigal, and what will bring him/her home. Help me not to question your methods but praise you as you work, even when it looks difficult knowing that suffering brings change. Please direct my prayers so they are in line with your desires. May thy will be done because you know best.

Light

"Search me, Oh God and know my heart: try me, and know my thoughts, And see if there be any wicked way in me, and lead me in the way everlasting." Psalm 139:23-24

Moving Forward

Sometimes our responsibility is being still, and not rescuing the prodigal through every trial, but offering prayer as we allow God to work.

DAY NINE – INSURMOUNTABLE

Truth Walk

Sometimes I feel like giving up. Packing it up and getting a one-way ticket to Maui. Waiting for the day the prodigal returns can seem long and overwhelming. I dream of going back to the 'good ole days' when things seemed better. The funny thing is, I'm not alone in this wistful journey; others have done the same, God's chosen people.

The Hebrew people were about two years into their journey when they reached the land God had promised them. We read in Numbers 13 that the Lord called upon Moses to spy out the land by picking a leader from each of the tribes of Israel. Their job was to check on the size and number of people in the region, what the cities were like, and if they were fortified. They were to check on the fruit of the land and bring back samples for tasting. But after a 40-day trek and back they returned discouraged. The men complained saying, "We went into the land where you sent us; and it certainly does flow with milk and honey, and this is its fruit. Nevertheless, the people who live in the land are strong, and the cities are fortified and very large; and moreover, we saw the descendants of Anak there." A few verses later the men proclaimed, "We are not able to go up against the people, for they are too strong for us." Only two men, Joshua and Caleb wanted to go forward and take the land God had promised. The others had another plan, "Let us appoint a leader and return to Egypt."

Fortunately, their one-way ticket back to Egypt fell through, but still, fear won out and they took another 38 years roaming the desert before trying again. I had to ask myself, why did God ask Moses to send the spies? God must have known the optics of a land too harsh and a people too big to conquer. He must have known they would become discouraged.

But then it occurred to me that this same group had already witnessed the impossible and beat the odds before:

- Pharaoh was too stubborn to let them go, and then the plagues came.
- Pharaoh's army was too fast to outrun, and then the sea parted.
- The desert elements were too harsh to overcome, and then the manna rained from the sky.
- The people were too many to lead, and then the cloud appeared to guide.

When they reached the Promised Land for the second time, God sent them to see the impossible again, but this time they chose to trust and obey. This time was different; they wanted to do this God's way.

It is the same with me. My God loves me and purposely sends me into overwhelming circumstances that are far beyond my ability to survive. And guess what? He is there taking me through every single struggle, trial, and tragedy. He walks me through things I can never endure on my own. He brings me successes that are far beyond my ability and bestows blessings upon me that I do not deserve.

All along I have been asking God to make me stronger, to endure this time of waiting for the prodigal, and thinking that somewhere inside of me there was this strength to rise up and conquer. Instead, I have met my impenetrable land. One that I cannot take alone, one that beckons me to remember all of the impossible situations God has miraculously brought me through. Just like the Hebrews, going backwards would be foolish and lead to a longer journey. Just like the Hebrews, I can only survive this ordeal by trusting God, nothing more, nothing less. It's His battle to win, on my own strength I will surely fail. With God anything is possible.

Prayer

Dear Lord, thank you for leading me into deep waters that is far beyond my ability to overcome. Thank you that this trial that will build my faith in you. Thank you for reminding me of all the times you came and rescued me and brought me your peace, even in the middle of the storm. Amen

Light

"But Moses said to the people, "Do not fear! Stand by and see the salvation of the Lord which He will accomplish for you today; for the Egyptians whom you have seen today, you will never see them again forever." Exodus 14:13

Moving Forward

Make a list of all the ways God has shown his faithfulness to you in the past.

DAY TEN - SAME PAGE

Truth Walk

When I was a child, I knew who to come to for permission depending on the ask. For instance, asking Mom to stay up late at night was out of the question, but Dad was cool with it. Asking Dad for money was probably not profitable, but Mom was a great ATM. Mom and Dad were not always on the same page or shared the same details regarding childrearing. It's the same with our prodigals.

The response to a prodigal's decisions and behaviors is often different for each family member. Even the way grief is processed can be expressed in various ways. This sometimes creates a large rift in family relationships, especially between husband and wife. One spouse may demand more intervention in the life of the prodigal, while the other believes in allowing consequences to be played out. Neither are wrong, but the lack of finding common ground can become the devil's playground. He's done it before.

In Genesis 27:5-17 we read about Isaac and Rebekah, parents of two very challenging children, but their oldest twin, Esau, is easily marked as the prodigal. He was irresponsible, selling his valuable birthright to his younger brother for a meal, and then marrying two women from a pagan culture. It was no wonder his mother was especially concerned. When it came time for Esau to receive the blessing as the oldest child, Rabekah decided to intervene, even to the point of deceiving her husband.

We read how Rebekah had Jacob dress up as his brother to fool his ailing and almost blind father, and it worked. Esau was so disappointed in losing his blessings that he swore to take his brother, Jacob's life. Rebekah realized all too soon that her plan didn't have the intended outcome, since she lost the relationship with both of her children, as well as her husband's trust.

When situations become very difficult, like managing a prodigal, mothers and fathers become desperate and act in rash ways they never normally consider. There is a belief in their power to manipulate circumstances and "fix" what is broken. Sometimes parents of prodigals will demand things from each other that are unreasonable, and sometimes impossible. Emotions can run high, relationships that were solid begin to crumble, and both start questioning the sovereignty of God.

It is at these times when parents of the prodigal need to acknowledge this battle before them has nothing to do with each other, it is spiritual. Their true mutual enemies are ruthless spiritual forces of darkness, and they know how to win, by dividing and conquering. So, what are these spiritual forces afraid of? Basically, you and your spouse as a united front with God in your midst. In Matthew 18:20 we read, For where two or three have gathered together in My name, I am there in their midst." We read in James 5:16, "Therefore, confess your sins to one another, and pray for one another so that you may be healed. The effective prayer of a righteous man can accomplish much." And in Ecclesiastes 4:9-12, "Two are better than one because they have a good return for their labor. For if either of them falls, the one will lift up his companion. But woe to the one who falls when there is not another to lift him up. Furthermore, if two lie down together they keep warm, but how can one be warm alone? And if one can overpower him who is alone, two can resist him. A cord of three strands is not quickly torn apart."

Your enemy, the Devil does not want you gathered with the Lord's power behind you; your enemy doesn't want you confessing together how you are struggling or praying for each other; and he definitely doesn't want you accomplishing much. He wants to get both of you alone on different paths, and then trip you up without a helping hand. Your enemy is keenly aware If you both unite under the Lord's direction, and remain obedient to God, then Satan loses. Rather, this season of life can surprisingly work to strengthen your marriage relationship according to another promise by a good God who says in Romans 8:28, "And we know that God causes all things to work together for good to those who love God, to those who are called according to *His* purpose."

Prayer

Dear Lord, I have struggled with a desire to find blame for this pain I'm going through. Many times, I've held others accountable instead of acknowledging that this is the broken side of heaven and we are all terribly flawed. Help me to stand on the side of righteousness and surrender control to the only one who actually possesses it. Let me trust in you, and support those who suffer as I do. Amen

Light

"Now may the God who gives perseverance and encouragement grant you to be of the same mind with one another according to Christ Jesus." Romans 15:5

Moving Forward

As Husband and Wife, make sure that you end the day praying for each other as you struggle through this time, asking for God's wisdom, and praying for your prodigal to come home.

DAY ELEVEN - THE RETURN

Truth Walk

My prodigal might be returning home, and I'm terrified. It's probably not for the reason you think. I'm afraid of losing what years of suffering have achieved in my life. When I look back on who I was and where I am today, the fear and trembling of salvation work harvested by a Holy God is truly remarkable. I never want to return to who I once was. I don't want to crawl off the altar of my living sacrifice, I want to continue flourishing in the glory of my Lord's accomplishments. I also want to refrain from attempting to control a narrative, to force what I think is best as I did before. I don't want to live in the constant uncertainty and fear that plagued my daily walk. I don't wish to wake up frozen by the accusations of the evil one who felt comfortable in my head. I don't want to bow again to the idol of Lynne, who tries to usurp the God I love, who alone determines my destiny. My fears resonated with the old hymn writer Robert Robinson, "Prone to wander Lord, I feel it." I cried out to God and told him that I fear my unreliable and impressionable flesh. He reminded me that he is stronger than my flesh.

It's not the first time he's had a tussle with human will, nor the ability to tame the beast within all of us. I'm reminded of Job, a man who feared God and turned from evil, yet in his flesh questioned the omniscient God about how he conducted business.

God responded accordingly-

> Then the Lord answered Job out of the whirlwind and said,
> "Who is this that darkens counsel
> By words without knowledge?
> "Now gird up your loins like a man,
> And I will ask you, and you instruct Me!
> "Where were you when I laid the foundation of the earth?
> Tell Me, if you have understanding,
> Who set its measurements? Since you know.
> Or who stretched the line on it?
> "On what were its bases sunk?
> Or who laid its cornerstone,
> When the morning stars sang together
> And all the sons of God shouted for joy?
> "Or who enclosed the sea with doors
> When, bursting forth, it went out from the womb;
> When I made a cloud its garment
> And thick darkness its swaddling band,
> And I placed boundaries on it
> And set a bolt and doors,
> And I said, 'Thus far you shall come, but no farther;
> And here shall your proud waves stop'?
> -Job 38:1-11

I'm reminded of Lot, Abraham's nephew, though considered righteous, became entangled in the wicked city of Sodom and its culture. God had to literally send angels to drag him and his family out. "When morning dawned, the angels urged Lot, saying, "Up, take your wife and your two daughters who are here, or you will be swept away in the punishment of the city." But he hesitated. So the men seized his hand and the hand of his wife and the hands of his two daughters, for the compassion of the Lord was upon him; and they brought him out, and put him outside the city. When they had brought them outside, one said, "Escape for your life! Do not look behind you, and do not stay anywhere in the valley; escape to the mountains, or you will be swept away." (Genesis 19:15-17)

In the New Testament I'm reminded of the Apostle Paul, who had an affliction and prayed for healing, but the one and only God who has our best in mind said, no. Paul writes it this way, "Because of the surpassing greatness of the revelations, for this reason, to keep me from exalting myself, there was given me a thorn in the flesh, a messenger of Satan to torment me—to keep me from exalting myself!" (2 Corinthians 12:7)

As the answer to my prayers for when my prodigal does return, I will trust in my Lord, and his ability to use whatever means necessary to conquer my flesh whether it be through suffering, discourse, supernatural events, or affliction. I will sing of the promises celebrated by hymn writer Wade Robinson (1890):

> Loved with everlasting love,
> drawn by grace that love to know,
> Spirit sent from Christ above,
> thou dost witness it is so.
> O this full and precious peace
> from his presence all divine;
> in a love that cannot cease,
> I am his and he is mine

Prayer

Dear Lord, Don't let me go back to the time when I relied on you less than I do now. I do not wish to be the fool spoken of in Proverbs 26:11, returning like a dog to his own vomit. Let me continue to live in the joy of the Lord. You are my strength, my portion, and my peace forever. Amen

Light

"What a wretched man I am! Who will rescue me from this body that is subject to death? Thanks be to God, who delivers me through Jesus Christ our Lord!" Romans 7:24

Moving Forward

When you feel the old life start to creep in follow the example set for us by Jesus who often retreated to be alone in prayer with the Father, for restoration and direction.

DAY TWELVE - THE BETRAYAL OF OTHERS

Truth Walk

I'm going to be honest; this was probably the most painful day in my devotional life when it came to my prodigal. I mourned that my prodigal was on a bad path and accepted the reality of betrayal toward our family, and the good sown. But I honestly had it in my head that surely those of faith, those that claim to walk with God, would point my prodigal in the right direction, God's direction. I was wrong.

It is painful to think that those who profess a godly life could be the ones to encourage and support a prodigal lifestyle. Some of them, even Christian leaders, will instead stand against you and support the sin of the prodigal. In today's culture many churches no longer speak out about unrighteousness, but instead harbor sinful practices in their congregation. Where are the shepherds? Leaders peddle the deception that, *it's okay to live as you wish, grace is enough; do whatever you want.* See how inclusive we are?

I'm wondering if they read what the apostle Paul had to say about accepting a professing Christian's sinful lifestyle?

"I wrote you in my letter not to associate with immoral people. I *did* not at all *mean* with the immoral people of this world, or with the covetous and swindlers, or with idolaters, for then you would have to go out of the world. But actually, I wrote to you not to associate with any so-called brother if he is an immoral person, or covetous, or an idolater, or a reviler, or a drunkard, or a swindler—not even to eat with such a one. For what have I to do with judging outsiders? Do you not judge those who are within *the church*? But those who are outside, God judges. Remove the wicked man from among yourselves." 1 Corinthians 5:9-13.

When is the last time those inside the church who were practicing immorality were removed? Of course I don't mean anyone who is struggling with sin, but walking knowingly, confidently, and unrepentant in sin? Instead, prodigals are given a big fluffy pillow of "acceptance." Why should they repent? There is no obvious need. It's the same feeling you get when you tell a teen his/her social media post is inappropriate and he/she responds with, "Hey I have 500 likes I must be okay!" In this case the big "Like" is from the those who claim faith in God and say they stand on God's word, the Bible.

Jesus had a hard time with this too. Upon approaching the temple during passion week Jesus saw merchants using the celebration of Passover as an opportunity to overcharge and defraud citizens who came to worship God. Instead of giving it a thumbs up, Jesus, feeling appalled, drove them out and flipped tables. Jesus proclaimed, "'My house shall be called a house of prayer,' but you make it a den of robbers." Hard to hear, but the truth. When I read about Jesus' passion for truth and justice, I'm reminded, what might be lacking from the pulpit is never absent from God's word. Unfortunately, there will always be a venue for those who want to walk in their own ways. In 2 Timothy 4:3 we read, *"For the time will come when they will not endure sound doctrine; but wanting to have their ears tickled, they will accumulate for themselves teachers in accordance to their own desires."*

You see prodigals will seek out those who will tell them exactly what they want to hear, and they will avoid truth tellers at all costs. So, what is the proper response? I pray for situations where my prodigal will be placed in the presence of someone who loves him/her enough to tell the truth.

My other response is to delve into scripture for my own wellbeing, so that the truth I stand on isn't my own opinion, I too need to avoid those who rob me of the truth when I am most vulnerable. You see the rain is falling, the floods in my life have come, the winds are blowing and slamming against my house, but I stand firm, for my truth is founded on the Rock.

Prayer

Dear Lord, I trust not in people or institutions that will surely let me down, I trust in your word. Please cause my prodigal to be placed among people who will speak the whole truth of your word into his/her life. Also speak truth into my life, you are the only one who will never betray me or let me down. To you belongs the glory forever. Amen

Light

"But Jesus, on His part, was not entrusting Himself to them, for He knew all men, and because He did not need anyone to testify concerning man, for He Himself knew what was in man." John 2:24-25

Moving Forward

Realize that you are not alone; Jesus was betrayed by all his disciples who fled him when he needed them the most. Pray for those who are deceived by the prodigal's charm, and that truth is revealed in their own life. Find a few close friends or a prodigal support group to share your prodigal struggles with, not for the purpose of slander, but to ask for prayer when you feel alone in your convictions to follow God and stand for righteousness.

DAY THIRTEEN - MY STORY

Truth Walk

It was a sad story. We sat in our Bible study group as one of the ladies tearfully confessed to ending a 20 year affair with a married man. Of course we grieved the betrayal, but we were also thankful for her repentance from adultery. The ultimate price was the lost years coveting a life she was never meant to have. What a waste of precious time!

One of the great temptations as the parent of a prodigal is to covet another person's life. I look at another mom who I believe is living the life I thought I'd be living at this time. This might be the joys of grand-parenting, or holiday celebrations that others enjoy that are not a part of my current experience. Still, I don't want to be caught wasting my years wishing for something the Lord has not currently planned for me to have.

It helps to remember that my life really isn't mine at all. In Romans 12:1 it says, "Therefore I urge you brethren, by the mercies of God, to present your bodies a living and holy sacrifice, acceptable to God which is your spiritual service of worship."

We all get the idea that we are to lay down what we want, and instead dedicate our life to living it God's way. But the real power of this command is revealed when we read the previous chapter that led to "Therefore." It goes like this-

"Oh the depth of the riches both on the wisdom and

knowledge of God! How unsearchable are his judgments and unfathomable his ways! For who has known the mind of the Lord, or who became his counselor?"

I don't know why I've been chosen to walk this path, but what I do know is that my God is generous with his riches, that he is wise and knowledgeable, that his ways are not conceivable with the limited faculties I possess, and that I don't have the foresight to counsel the God of the universe on how things should go. Better said, "Who am I to question God?"

Fortunately, I've been given a role model to follow when it comes to accepting a change of plans. A young Jewish girl betrothed to her beloved was planning a beautiful wedding when her plans were drastically altered. Her sweet marriage would instead be shrouded in scandal; her newlywed year spent traveling in brutal conditions while pregnant; Not long after she would be seeking asylum in another country. It's Mary, the mother of our Lord. So what was her response when the Angel showed up to announce this life altering plan?

"Behold the bondslave of the Lord; may it be done to me according to your word." Luke 1:38

It's clear to me in this passage that Mary had already defined who she was, a bondservant who existed for the purpose of the Master. She disregarded "self" and was willing to be at the disposal of her God. It was not about her desires at all. A few verses later we see that she is able, even at such a young age, to grasp what is called "the eternal perspective."

"And my spirit has rejoiced in God my Savior. For he has had regard for the humble state of his bondslave; For behold this time on all generations will count me blessed." Luke 1:47-48

It's clear that my satisfaction in life cannot come from what I construe to be fair, or to wish for circumstances different from what the Lord has chosen for me. After all, this isn't a life gone array. This is my ordained life, guided and directed by Almighty God. To covet that "other" is to miss out on the blessings that are before me. My beautiful story is unfolding.

Prayer

Dear Lord, thank you for knowing my future and what is best. I cannot see what is up ahead, but like Mary, let my soul rejoice in knowing that you chose me for this task of praying and waiting for a prodigal. Let me lay down what I want, and gracefully receive and then rejoice over your proclamation upon my life, my Lord and my Savior. Amen

Light

"For the Mighty One has done great things for me; And holy is His name. And His mercy is upon generation after generation toward those who fear Him." Luke 1:49-50.

Moving Forward

One of my favorite things to do is read and watch biographies on people who were underdogs that overcame difficult circumstances to succeed. I am aware that God is writing my biography, and the blessings for me and my family are in the hands of a loving and powerful God.

DAY FOURTEEN
- GRIEVING

Truth Walk

Back in my hometown there are two mothers grieving over the loss of their children. It's heartbreaking. Both losses involved car accidents. While it was beautiful to watch the community circle around them with love and support, it occurred to me that my loss, that of losing a child to a prodigal lifestyle, is to be experienced without a great deal of support. Of course there is hope of a sooner reunion in my case, so it's no comparison in that respect, but often parents of prodigals feel as though they must suffer in silence.

When you speak the words "I have a prodigal" to others you often risk the response of judgment. You are aware of the thoughts of, "I wonder what they did wrong as a parent," appears as the pink elephant in the room. Sometimes we are silent so as not to slander or bring undue shame on the prodigal. She/He is my child, and my natural inclination is to protect and make sure the return is congenial. We want to provide a way home and create a path filled with grace steps not poisonous barbs. I want my prodigal to know the door to redemption with his/her God, and earthly family is wide open.

People often associate the act of grieving with physical death, but let's face it losing your prodigal feels like a death, and it is. Your dreams of what was to be will never materialize as you imagined it. There are many kinds of griefs associated with prodigals: the loss of innocence, missing milestones like graduation, weddings, holidays and birthdays, the relationship itself, and missing shared life experiences. I'm not saying that God can't heal or use what is broken, but it will never be the same on this side of eternity the way you imagined.

This is true for all of us. When we make decisions that are less than what God intended for us we are forced to reap the consequences. In scripture we read how King Saul made decisions that cost him the legacy of his monarchy, and Moses' anger cost him a journey into the Promised Land.

Fortunately, short comings on our part do not hamper the sovereignty of God's plans. God is in the business of using brokenness. God forgave King David for his adultery; Jesus met and freed the woman with five husbands at the well; Jesus stopped the stoning of the adulteress in the city square. God even used a man, previously named Saul, a persecutor of Christians, to write a great deal of the New Testament. Our God is into redemption.

We all know of modern-day prodigals that have returned to God and now minister to others in amazing ways. He is the God who in time makes all things new as proclaimed in Joel 2:25, "I will make up to you for the years That the swarming locust has eaten", and in Ezekiel 37:4-6 we read, "Again He said to me, "Prophesy over these bones and say to them, 'O dry bones, hear the word of the Lord.' Thus says the Lord God to these bones, 'Behold, I will cause breath to enter you that you may come to life. I will put sinews on you, make flesh grow back on you, cover you with skin and put breath in you that you may come alive; and you will know that I am the Lord."

It's normal to grieve, believe me I understand, but it's more important to not wallow indefinitely in grief when God wants to move us on toward a bigger plan. If we are not careful, we can, ironically, become the prodigal ourselves, fighting God about how he chooses to deal with our situation. Instead, join God's revised story for your prodigal, but more importantly join God in his revised plan for you. He is not finished with your story and will use the grieving process to achieve his perfect plan. We acknowledge, as Job did in Job 42:2 regarding the omnipotence of God, "I know that You can do all things, And that no purpose of Yours can be thwarted."

Prayer

Dear Lord, Thank you for not leaving me to grieve alone. I might experience the death of my dream, but you dream bigger than I can ever imagine. You are the one who restores what is broken; you are the one who will repay for the years the locusts have eaten. I choose to trust you on this journey. Make me your willing sacrifice, may I be pleasing to you. Amen

Light

"He heals the brokenhearted and binds up their wounds." Psalm 147:3

Moving Forward

Allow yourself a healthy time to grieve and if needed get some professional support from a Christian therapist. Here is one resource to consider https://www.christiancounselorsnetwork.com/

DAY FIFTEEN - THE FRUIT

Truth Walk

I grew up in California's Central Valley where you can't help but become familiar with farming. My family was not a farming family, but with five acres to manage we became educated about some basics. The responsibility to move pasture pipes from one side of the field to the other fell upon my brother and me. It was hard work keeping the fields green for our horse and a steer named Freezer Beef. Later, my own family lived across the street from an almond orchard. Harvest time with its dust and heavy equipment is something to behold. I remember a friend from church who would work during harvest as a cantaloupe fruit inspector on the assembly line. It gave me an appreciation for those who knew how to properly inspect fruit, so the good stuff hit the market.

Fruit is something God often talks about in the Bible. In Psalm 1:3 he explains the benefits of those who delight in God's laws, "But his delight is in the law of the Lord, And in His law he meditates day and night. He will be like a tree firmly planted by streams of water, Which yields its fruit in its season And its leaf does not wither; And in whatever he does, he prospers."

In Psalm 92:14-15 we read how aging doesn't limit productivity for the righteous, "They will still yield fruit in old age; They shall be full of sap and very green, To declare that the Lord is upright; He is my rock, and there is no unrighteousness in Him."

Jesus often used fruit in his parables as a metaphor, equating them with the physical harvest of the heart's condition. Jesus even charges us to become fruit inspectors, and most of us are pretty good at it. That is, we are great at noticing others' fruit, not so astute at analyzing our own. In Matthew 7:15 we are to recognize false teachers by judging them according to the fruit produced in their lives. In Matthew 7:4 we are warned to use the same measuring stick for ourselves that we use to judge others. "You hypocrite, first take the plank out of your own eye, and then you will see clearly to remove the speck from your brother's eye." After this completed self-assessment, the goal is still speck removing in order to restore a fellow believer from a sinful lifestyle.

It's very clear, fruit is important. The scriptures say it this way, "For there is no good tree which produces bad fruit, nor, on the other hand, a bad tree which produces good fruit. For each tree is known by its own fruit. For men do not gather figs from thorns, nor do they pick grapes from a briar bush. The good man out of the good treasure of his heart brings forth what is good; and the evil man out of the evil treasure brings forth what is evil; for his mouth speaks from that which fills his heart. (Luke 6:43-45)

Oftentimes parents and friends of prodigals are frustrated when they expect to pick peaches but end up with a fist full of thistles. Many parents of prodigals will invest massive amounts of time and money to correct the behaviors of their children instead of investing in the real issue. This is because we focus on the words themselves, (and the behaviors that follow), instead of seeing them as a barometer of the deeper issue of the heart. Remember "man looks on the outward appearance, but the Lord looks on the heart." (1 Samuel 16:7).

Cultivating fruit isn't easy, just like deciding when, or if we should intervene to help a prodigal. Sure, the father of the prodigal in Luke 15 could have forced him into rehab or therapy, but it would have been a temporary fix until the prodigal had a change of heart. This doesn't mean we abandon the prodigal who cries out for help, but repentance, and a desire for change, needs to precede action for true healing to take place. If it doesn't, you might inadvertently be harvesting more thornbushes.

Prayer

Dear Lord, we love our prodigals so much that no cost is too high for us to bring them back, yet we know only you can bring our prodigal to repentance. Let us be like you Lord, not focusing on cleaning up the outside, but instead rely upon the power of God to change the prodigal heart. Lord give us wisdom in our decision-making, as well as strength to wait for your timing. Thank you for showing us the current manifestations of the prodigal heart, so that we know how to better pray for his or her soul. Amen.

Light

"I am the vine, you are the branches; he who abides in Me and I in him, he bears much fruit, for apart from Me you can do nothing." John 15:5

Moving Forward

When praying ask God to reveal the inner struggle of the heart of your prodigal. Allow the Holy Spirit to direct the details of how to pray in faith for heart changes.

DAY SIXTEEN – IN CHARGE

Truth Walk

Those who have committed their life to Christ expect difficulty. When you first come to the Lord there's that initial rush of rejoicing and celebrating your rebirth from death to life. You are so grateful you want to shout it from the rooftops! But then trials come, and eventually you realize the spiritual battle set before you, and it's hard. It almost appears the greater your successes the more the attacks come.

As humans we cannot see the spiritual warfare that surrounds us on all fronts. Ephesians 6:12, says it this way, "For our struggle is not against flesh and blood, but against the rulers, against the powers, against the world forces of this darkness, against the spiritual forces of wickedness in the heavenly places."

There are things in the spiritual world that we cannot see clearly with our human eyes. In Job 4:12-15, the messenger Eliphaz relates a spiritual visitation, "Now a word was brought to me stealthily,And my ear received a whisper of it. "Amid disquieting thoughts from the visions of the night, When deep sleep falls on men, Dread came upon me, and trembling, And made all my bones shake. "Then a spirit passed by my face; The hair of my flesh bristled up."

In Matthew 8:29-31, Jesus deals with men who have demonic spirits within them crying out, "What business do we have with each other, Son of God? Have You come here to torment us before the time?" Now there was a herd of many swine feeding at a distance from them. The demons *began* to entreat Him, saying, "If You *are going* to cast us out, send us into the herd of swine."

Throughout scripture we also witness holy spiritual forces called angelic beings, who make announcements and proclamations, fight, and protect. It was an angel named, Gabriel, sent to Mary to announce the birth of Jesus. In 2 Kings 6, the prophet Elisha is surrounded by an unseen mighty army of angels, "Then Elisha prayed and said, "O Lord, I pray, open his eyes that he may see." And the Lord opened the servant's eyes and he saw; and behold, the mountain was full of horses and chariots of fire all around Elisha."

As New Testament believers, our power to fight spiritual battles comes not only from outside angelic forces, but from our indwelling Holy Spirit. We read in Acts 1:8, "but you will receive power when the Holy Spirit has come upon you; and you shall be My witnesses both in Jerusalem, and in all Judea and Samaria, and even to the remotest part of the earth." In 1 John 4:4 we are taught not to fear evil because, "greater is He who is in you than he who is in the world."

But when you start thinking about the cost of discipleship and what you will gain versus what you lose, especially when it comes to a prodigal, it can be scary. I'm almost embarrassed to admit that I worried about the consequences of writing this book, pondering what the unseen "spiritual forces" will do to me. It was then I heard that small still voice from God say, "I alone am in charge of your suffering." You see God will decide what I need and don't need, Satan does not have jurisdiction over my soul, my suffering, or my life. The scriptures consistently show the boundaries God sets upon the spiritual realm. In the book of Job we see the limitations God puts upon Satan, "Behold, all that he has is in your power, only do not put forth your hand on him." So Satan departed from the presence of the Lord." In the New Testament we again see the demand of evil upon the apostle Peter, "Simon, Simon, behold, Satan has demanded permission to sift you like wheat; but I have prayed for you, that your faith may not fail; and you, when once you have turned again, strengthen your brothers" (Luke 22:31-32).

We have an all-powerful God who is standing up for us, praying for us, interceding for us. No matter what befalls us we will stand firm, evil is no match for our Holy God, even when it comes to our commitment to love our prodigals and pray for their return.

Prayer

Dear Lord, We know that we fight a battle we cannot see with human eyes. Give us spiritual eyes to see and pray with confidence for your glory to be revealed in our lives and in the lives of our precious prodigal.

Light

"What, then, shall we say in response to these things? If God is for us, who can be against us? He who did not spare his own Son, but gave him up for us all—how will he not also, along with him, graciously give us all things?" Romans 8:31-32

Moving Forward

Do not be threatened by the enemy, you are on Holy Ground that God has already taken. Speak truth from your lips when you arise each morning. Thank God for the suffering he chooses for you and trust him to carry out his promises.

DAY SEVENTEEN - CELEBRATING SIN

Truth Walk

Those who love prodigals walk a very tight rope. We struggle to find the proper and balanced response to prodigal behaviors. We don't agree with deeds antithetical to our Christian walk, yet we love the prodigal despite those behaviors. It can be difficult to navigate. Sometimes in our effort to maintain the peace, lines are crossed, and if not careful, we capitulate to the very things God says, "no" to. This is not a new problem, the Apostle Paul had to address one such issue in the church of Corinth. There was a couple in church who had an immoral relationship. It was wrong and everyone knew it, but they had a lot of money and power, and hey, at least they came to church, right? Perhaps the church wanted to be seen as *loving* and *accepting*. For them, it was an example of how tolerant believers can be. The only problem? It was wrong, and the Apostle Paul was quick to condemn the "unity at any cost" narrative. In 1 Corinthias 5:2, Paul writes, "You have become arrogant and have not mourned instead, so that the one who had done this deed would be removed from your midst."

Paul's reasoning for excommunication is quite clear in 1 Corinthians 5:5, "I have decided to deliver such a one to Satan for the destruction of his flesh, so that his spirit may be saved in the day of the Lord Jesus." The goal wasn't to punish for punishment's sake but rather allowing suffering and shame to bring forth repentance and salvation.

Today's church also struggles with how to respond to open sin. Likewise, how we respond to our prodigals, who at one time professed faith, but now live in rebellion to God, is important. Many parents will say, "We are trying to love them well so they will come back." But is it really love?

In 1 Corinthians 13:6 we see a very important element of love, as defined by scripture, "does not rejoice in unrighteousness, but rejoices with the truth;" Yet how many Christian parents "rejoice" at celebrations or situations that are not honored by God? Are they celebrating and rejoicing in truth? Or celebrating lies, depravity, and false doctrine? What we often see is not love at all according to scripture, so what is it? Paul called it arrogance and the refusal to mourn the sin. Arrogance because we have decided in our hubris to redefine what God has already said. It is refusal to mourn when we are focused either upon our own suffering and discomfort that obedience requires, or an attempt to shield any subsequent discomfort to the disobedient prodigal. If today's churches and families are capitulating to the world's definition of love, or worse rewriting God's love, how are we any different from the disobedient church Paul rebuked?

Jesus calls us out of cultural compromise by stating plainly the cost of discipleship. "Do not think that I came to bring peace on the earth; I did not come to bring peace, but a sword. For I came to set a man against his father, and a daughter against her mother, and a daughter-in-law against her mother-in-law; and a man's enemies will be the members of his household. He who loves father or mother more than Me is not worthy of Me; and he who loves son or daughter more than Me is not worthy of Me. And he who does not take his cross and follow after Me is not worthy of Me. He who has found his life will lose it, and he who has lost his life for My sake will find it." Matthew 10:34-39.

If our lifestyle decisions exemplify compromise, then it shouldn't surprise us when the prodigal doesn't take our convictions about God seriously. They notice when actions don't match convictions. True, prodigals might not agree with our pursuit for righteousness at any cost, but they for sure won't value a faith that is built upon convenience. Equally challenging for the prodigal is when we are not clear about how we ourselves ought to live regarding the choices we make.

I once heard Pastor Vodie Bauchman say something that has truly challenged the way I process my decision-making, it helps me strip away any pretense, intentional or unintentional. Pastor Bauchman says, "*Finish the sentence* and then you will understand what you are really saying."

Let's apply this method regarding the prodigal:

Decision: "I need to support my prodigal."
Finish the sentence: "I need to support my prodigal even if it means encouraging sinful choices that will continue to heap judgment upon him/her and delay any repentance that might lead to salvation or restoration." (Well that makes it clear).

Realize it works both ways-

Decision: I will stand against the decision my prodigal has made.
Finish the sentence: I will stand against the unrighteous decision my prodigal has made because I love him/her too much to lie or pretend that this bad decision will be for his/her good."

This kind of processing brings great clarity to situations that appear *kind* on the outside, but are both deceptive, and counterproductive to God's plan for redemption. Similarly, this process can ferret out worldly beliefs that proclaim, "standing on truth is cruel", when it is really "true love" in action. Perhaps the best part of this honest love is "patience" which is walking in obedience as a faithful witness, while we wait for God to move, using whatever methods He deems necessary to bring the prodigal home.

Prayer

Dear Lord, Thank you for helping me mourn as I remain steadfast to your principles and your truth. Please let me love with truth and kindness as defined by a loving God and not a rotting and depraved culture. Let me remain humble and act becomingly as a believer who is unashamed of the gospel of truth, regardless of how others respond. Above all don't allow me to support and rejoice in things that scripture forbids and breaks the heart of God. Amen

Light

"...and although they know the ordinance of God, that those who practice such things are worthy of death, they not only do the same, but also give hearty approval to those who practice them." Romans 1:32

Moving Forward

Work on processing your actions regarding your prodigal by "finishing the sentence" as a way to measure your motives and avoid behavior that contradicts your commitment to living righteously.

DAY EIGHTEEN - SABATOGE

Truth Talk

Shame: a condition of humiliating disgrace or disrepute.

Family and friends of prodigals are embarrassed. We are desperately afraid that people on the outside will look at the prodigal and think the behaviors reflect us. "Is his/her mom okay with him/ her wearing such scanty clothes on social media?" "Was he/she not taught proper manners?" "What kind of family is this anyway?" "I wonder if they use those kinds of words in their home."

Why are we consumed with shame? Because all of us fall victim to this kind of thinking. The universal belief is that a person is a direct reflection of who raises or influences them, good or bad. But just like any worldly belief there are partial truths mixed in with a whole bunch of lies. Let us look to one example that tosses a monkey wrench into the "you are who raised you philosophy."

In 1 Samuel we are introduced to Hannah, a barren woman who is married to Elkanah. Hannah is depressed because she could not have children whereas her husband's other wife, (*he had two*), Peninnah, produced several children. Hannah cried out to God for a child and vowed to dedicate him to the Lord all the days of his life. God blessed her with a son named Samuel, and true to her word, she brought the boy to the priest Eli for him to raise to do the Lord's work.

Samuel grew to become a godly man, being a spiritual guide to kings and those in authority. By now you are thinking well of course he was godly he was raised by a priest; Eli must have been a great influence on him. But then you learn about Eli's biological prodigy. Both of Eli's sons turned out to be prodigals, the scriptures call them scoundrels. So how does one square with that? The reality is that people get to choose, and other people get to judge, but the evidence doesn't always square with the condemnation. Are there other God-fearing folks connected with prodigals? The list is long, here are a few:

Parents: Adam & Eve, (Genesis chapter 4)
Prodigal: Cain

Parents: Manoah and his wife (Judges chapters 13-16)
Prodigal: Sampson

Parents: King David & Ahinoam (2 Samuel 13)
Prodigal: Amnon

Parents: Jacob (Israel) & Wives (Genesis 37)
Prodigals: Reuben, Simeon, Levi, Judah, Dan, Nephtali, Gad, Issachar, Asher, Zebulan

Parent: God (Romans 3:23)
Prodigals: Every human born

The truth is the enemy of God, (Satan), wants to keep you in a state of isolation and embarrassment, because doing so will neutralize you from doing God's work. This idea however presupposes that God only uses the equipped, the famous, the social elites, and those who have their ducks in a row. But scripture shows otherwise. Even God choosing the Jewish nation to fulfill his promises isn't built upon their great presence, in Deuteronomy

7:7 we read, "The Lord did not set His love on you nor choose you because you were more in number than any of the peoples, for you were the fewest of all peoples." In Judges 6:15, it was Gideon himself reminding God how ill-equipped he would be as a warrior as the least impressive family in town, and the youngest male. In Acts 4:13, the educated elite in the church couldn't understand how two fishermen from Galilee were so poised and articulate, "Now as they observed the confidence of Peter and John and understood that they were uneducated and untrained men, they were amazed, and *began* to recognize them as having been with Jesus." Shall I continue? God used a felon (Moses) to lead the Children of Israel, a beauty queen (Esther) to save her people, and a repentant murderer (the Apostle Paul) to write a large portion of the New Testament. Let's be honest, God uses the unqualified for his purposes, if not, who would be left to work with?

But if we believe that we are "tarnished" by the prodigal's behavior we are buying into lies. The first lie is that we need to be perfect to serve. No one fits that description. Secondly, we do not serve because of our family's goodness, Christ alone is our righteousness. And lastly, we can't look to people to defend our name and reputation, it is the Lord who does that. Our best example to follow is Jesus, a man despised and forsaken of men, yet he set his face to the work of the cross regardless of the prodigal children who had forsaken Him.

Prayer

Dear Lord, if I constantly gaze upon my prodigal, I am not fixing my eyes upon you, the author and perfector of my faith. Let me not get distracted from accomplishing the good works you have prepared for me to do. Amen

Light

But the Lord is my defense; and my God is the rock of my refuge. Psalm 94:22

Moving Forward

Don't hang out on your prodigal's social media page or waste time playing the detective trying to find out his/her latest problem. Focus on the good work you are supposed to do now. When others point out bad behaviors of your prodigal just respond by saying, "Thank you for your continued prayers," and leave it there.

DAY NINETEEN - DISCIPLINE

Truth Talk

Discipline - Training expected to produce a specific character or pattern of behavior, especially training that produces moral or mental improvement.

Discipline is hard. It's the part of us that needs to be changed or managed in a better way. When given the choice of whether or not to receive discipline we would resist it at every turn. We are masters of excuses, creating diversions and downright avoidance. But when we are forced to acquire discipline, it is uncomfortable yet necessary.

As believers in Christ, we are to pursue righteousness, but the pursuit of righteousness hinges upon our ability to develop discipline. Take 2 Timothy 2:22, "Now flee from youthful lusts and pursue righteousness, faith, love *and* peace, with those who call on the Lord from a pure heart." Here it takes discipline to flee youthful lust and put forth effort to seek after faith, love and peace. In Hebrews 12:1, we read, "Therefore, since we have so great a cloud of witnesses surrounding us, let us also lay aside every encumbrance and the sin which so easily entangles us, and let us run with endurance the race that is set before us." In this verse we recognize that discipline requires us to walk away from sin and anything that gets in the way of our race toward righteousness.

Fortunately, we are not alone in our pursuit of righteousness because we have a God that knows exactly how to produce discipline. Scripture says, "For those whom the Lord loves he disciplines, and He scourges every son whom He receives." (Hebrews 12:6). In Revelation 3:19 it's put this way, "Those whom I love, I reprove and discipline; therefore be zealous and repent."

This particular call to repent in the book of Revelations is directed toward members in churches that are not correctly living out their calling. Their decisions and behavior, or lack of, required the Lord to discipline them and call them to repent. What exactly do churches need to repent of? It depends on the church:

Church in Ephesus
- Repent for: Lost the initial love they had for God
- Consequence: Lose their influence

Church in Pergamum
- Repent for: False teaching and sexual immorality and idol worship
- Consequence: False teachers will be destroyed

Church in Thyatira
- Repent for: Tolerance of evil leader and sexual immorality, and idol worship.
- Consequence: Suffering for false leader, punish those who participate in her evil, strike the children dead.

Church in Sardis
- Repent for: Unfinished deeds
- Consequence: Be discovered when God returns

Church in Laodicea
- Repent for: Indifference to God's calling
- Consequence: Spewed out of the mouth of God

After reviewing this list, I was surprised. While some churches were engaging in outright sin such as idolatry, sexual immorality and false teaching, others were disciplined for lack of godly commitment, not doing the deeds God called them to, and their indifference to God. All actions, active or passive, were equally called out as sin, and required repentance. This led me to recognize my own need for discipline. As I walk the road as the prodigal parent, I have realized that the Lord is using his disciplining love on me just as much as my prodigal. I have areas of my life that are broken, and if I'm not careful the lack in my life gets clouded by the lack in my child's life. I can focus all day long on what my prodigal is doing wrong, but the only thing accomplished is building up logs for my own eyes. This obsession to focus on the prodigal and not me is a great deviation from my own self-reflection. My time would be better served if I focused on what the Lord is doing in my life and where I fall short.

Besides, we know the same great love that the Lord has while on a mission to discipline me, is the same one he has for the prodigal. Perhaps a more correct prayer is, "Lord please continue to love my prodigal."

My therapist husband would say the pathway to change is discomfort. We only change when things are uncomfortable or if we want something really, really bad. In the case of my prodigal, I am uncomfortable with the situation, and I really, really, want a restored relationship under God. So perhaps this event is just the kind of discomfort I needed to make some changes in my own life. Maybe just maybe there are some missed steps in my own life that require reflection and change. I know one thing for sure; God loves me and is committed to helping me change by disciplining me and scourging me if needed. I will not remain the same after this difficulty, I will be blessed.

Prayer

Dear Lord, I have areas in my life that need change. I invite you into those areas to love me with your rebuke, your scourging, and your discipline. I trust in you to bring forth the repentance needed so that I can pursue righteousness unencumbered, not weighted down with sin or disobedience. Thank you for loving me well, as you love my prodigal with that same commitment to bring forth faith, love, and peace. Amen.

Light

Behold, how happy is the man whom God reproves, So do not despise the discipline of the Almighty. Job 5:17

Moving Forward

Look into areas where God is requiring change in your life. Thank him for struggles that force you to lean on God and change.

DAY TWENTY - YOU ARE A GIFT

Truth Talk

Godly parents love their children. They embrace the truth of Psalm 127:3, "Behold, children are a gift of the Lord, The fruit of the womb is a reward." Mothers and Fathers, demonstrate this love in many ways. There are basic needs to be addressed, from feedings, to diaper changes, to midnight vigils over fevered brows. Sacrifices are made, and social events come second to family commitments, also, previous luxuries are traded in for a child's education and well-being. Goals are different, priorities change, and a nuclear family is created and enjoyed. But sometimes children grow up and instead of embracing the love and commitment modeled at home, they walk a path that is contrary to family life. Sometimes they walk away from God. It's not a new story. As a parent, you are in good company. The same disappointment is shared with the God of the Universe.

In the book of Jerimiah, chapter two, we read the words from God, who is mourning over the nation Israel who has walked away from him, despite his past provision and protection. His words sound similar to earthly parents dealing with the disappointment of a prodigal:

> ➤ *What fault did your ancestors find in me,*
> *that they strayed so far from me?*
> *They followed worthless idols*

> *and became worthless themselves.*
> ➤ *They did not ask, 'Where is the Lord,*
>   *who brought us up out of Egypt*
>   *and led us through the barren wilderness,*
>   *through a land of deserts and ravines,*
>   *a land of drought and utter darkness,*
>   *a land where no one travels and no one lives?'*
> ➤ *I brought you into a fertile land*
>   *to eat its fruit and rich produce.*
>   *But you came and defiled my land*
>   *and made my inheritance detestable.*
> ➤ *The priests did not ask,*
>   *'Where is the Lord?'*
>   *Those who deal with the law did not know me;*
>   *the leaders rebelled against me.*
>   *The prophets prophesied by Baal,*
>   *following worthless idols.*

You can almost hear the tears of disappointment in God's tone. His beautiful children of Israel had walked away. But God isn't done. He continues in his lament with typical parental warning, also something we parents are familiar with:

> · *Now why go to Egypt*
>   *to drink water from the Nile?*
>   *And why go to Assyria*
>   *to drink water from the Euphrates?*
>   *Your wickedness will punish you;*
>   *your backsliding will rebuke you.*
>   *Consider then and realize*
>   *how evil and bitter it is for you*
>   *when you forsake the Lord your God*
>   *and have no awe of me,"*
>   *declares the Lord, the Lord Almighty.*

So how does God end his rant? In verse 36 he says, "*Why do you go about so much, changing your ways? You will be disappointed by Egypt as you were by Assyria.*" God stands his ground on what is true, expressing quite articulately that false gods, and his children's fascination with a depraved culture will fail them, as will anything apart from the goodness of God. He knows what is

ahead of his prodigal and he wishes it could be different. Haven't we all been there? Yet, despite his anger, in Jeremiah 3:12 he calls the prodigal home, "Go and proclaim these words toward the north and say, 'Return, faithless Israel,' declares the Lord;
'I will not look upon you in anger. For I am gracious,' declares the Lord; 'I will not be angry forever."

You see parents who love the prodigal are a gift too. How do I know? Solomon the wisest man to ever live recorded the benefits of godly parents. "Hear, my son, your father's instruction And do not forsake your mother's teaching;" Proverbs 1:8

Parents who walk with God value what God values. And just like God, dealing with his prodigal, they too plead and warn; they mourn and are disappointed; they hope for change. But also like their Father, they know how to faithfully forgive.

Prayer

Dear Lord, thank you for the beautiful memories of raising my child, and the privilege to parent. Children are truly a blessing from the Lord. Thank you that in some small way I can experience the love of God for his children, his provision, his joys, his disappointments, and his never-ending compassion. Use my experiences to make me more like you. Show me areas in my life that I too am faithless and guide me to repentance and reconciliation with you. Amen

Light

So will My word be which goes forth from My mouth; It will not return to Me empty, Without accomplishing what I desire, And without succeeding in the matter for which I sent it. Isaiah 55:11

Moving Forward

Sometimes prodigal parents can feel like the commitment of child rearing was fruitless. It is never fruitless to obey God. Look at your previous sacrifices through the lens of events that helped mold you into the image of Christ. See it as a future opportunity to see God's word fulfilled.

DAY TWENTY-ONE - PRODUCTIVE SUFFERING

Truth Talk

I belong to a women's fellowship group that meets once a month for lunch. We encourage each other in our walk with God, pray, and share yummy recipes. During our lunch we read thought provoking questions that help us stay focused on what God is doing in each of our lives. On one occasion the question was, "Who has helped you the most in your walk with the Lord." I blurted out the answer and surprised even myself. "My prodigal." Why would so painful a relationship cause me to respond that way? Because it is true. Having a prodigal has forced me to do business with God. I've had to ask God the hard questions, I've had to do a lot of self-examination, and more importantly I've had to trust God in areas of great discomfort. I am not the same person who started out on this journey, and it makes perfect sense why. Rarely in life do easy things promote growth. It's tough things that test our metal, our faith. You don't have to delve too far into scripture to see how life's challenges brought about the most courageous actions in people's lives. Let's look at a few of them.

In the book of Genesis, we meet a man who is described as righteous and blameless, a man who walks with God. His name is Noah. While living in an evil and depraved culture, God called

Noah out to do something quite extraordinary; build a boat in the desert. Not just any boat, but the biggest boat ever built. Why? Because something huge was going to happen, something Noah wouldn't comprehend or see for 100 years. It's a big ask for sure. It's not lost on me that in the New Testament it took great faith for the apostle Peter to get out of the boat to walk on the water with Jesus, while here Noah is asked to faithfully build and get into the boat. And this challenge wasn't a quick "miracle by Tuesday" kind of situation, but long-suffering devotion to the task God required. It changed Noah, his family, and all of mankind forever.

In the book of Ruth, we meet a young woman from a pagan Moabite culture who marries into a family from Jewish faith. But before this couple can have children the husband dies. Ruth is left alone with two other widows, her Moabite sister-in-law and mother-in-law, Naomi. Then her Jewish mother-in-law decides to return to her home country and encourages Ruth to stay in Moab and start over. Ruth is at a crossroads. But something has changed, Ruth has fallen in love with her mother-in-law's God. And while walking into the unknown by following Naomi home is scary, the thought of returning to the old way feels even more frightening. Here words of transformation in the face of adversity ring clear,

"But Ruth said, "Do not urge me to leave you or turn back from following you; for where you go, I will go, and where you lodge, I will lodge. Your people shall be my people, and your God, my God." Ruth 1:16. Ruth bravely walks by faith, not by sight. It doesn't take long for God to reward her faithfulness with a husband and a family legacy of prophetic promise. Matthew 1:5 lists her husband Boaz in the lineage of Christ. Boaz had a mother, who like Ruth, left a pagan culture in Jerico, in trade for the One True God.

Let's also not forget Esther. The beauty queen who risked death by her husband, the king, to save her people from destruction. She had to conquer her fear and trust in the living God. And the list goes on. The scriptures are filled with people facing hard circumstances that required firm resolutions. Circumstances that changed them for the better. It's exactly as James 1:3-4 proclaims, "knowing that the testing of your faith produces endurance. And let endurance have its perfect result, so that you may be complete and lacking in nothing."

My prodigal trial has produced in me great resolve. Today my faith is more firmly rooted in God. I no longer trust in my own ability to manage trials; I trust in the God who will carry me through them and bring about the "perfect result" so I can be complete. Before I lacked, today I stand better equipped, relying on God's strength to get through this season.

If I fail to allow the prodigal experience to change me, but remain in fight, flight or anger mode, I will miss out. It reminds me of Mordecai's message to Esther when she was considering playing it safe and avoiding the opportunity to act on her faith, *"For if you remain silent at this time, relief and deliverance will arise from the Jews from another place and you and your father's house will perish."* Esther 4:14. God is a big God, and he will accomplish his purposes with or without me, but rather than miss out on what God is trying to teach me through the prodigal, I will choose to grab this season so God can use it to teach me, and make me mature; to be used by Him for such a time as this.

Prayer

Dear Lord, thank you for using the experience of waiting for my prodigal to force me to turn to you. You have torn open the weak spaces in my faith and brought light into dark places. I know this time of suffering is not wasted, as I trust in your faithfulness to make me complete and not lacking. Amen

Light

Blessed is a man who perseveres under trial; for once he has been approved, he will receive the crown of life which *the Lord* has promised to those who love Him. James 1:12

Moving Forward

Flee the pity party. Spend time thanking God for using the prodigal experience to bring about maturity in your own life. Praise God as you lean into the Lord, not only to survive this season, but thrive in it.

DAY TWENTY-TWO - IS MY PRODIGAL SAVED?

Truth Talk

When talking with those who love the prodigal, by far the most urgent concern is whether their prodigal is saved. It's a hard question. Many will cite young prayers and baptisms, others good deeds or church service; all could be evidence of the living faith through works as James 2:18 explains, "But someone may well say, "You have faith and I have works; show me your faith without the works, and I will show you my faith by my works."

But the word of God also describes in Matthew 7:22-23 the problem with pseudo works without a relationship with God, "Many will say to Me on that day, 'Lord, Lord, did we not prophesy in Your name, and in Your name cast out demons, and in Your name perform many miracles?' And then I will declare to them, 'I never knew you; depart from Me, you who practice lawlessness."

So which one is my prodigal? What is the response to such a crucial question? Truth is hard to hear, but we must live in truth to pray wisely and love well. Here are four truths:

Truth #1

I do not control the destiny of my prodigal's soul. It's a hard pill to swallow, but my prodigal's salvation isn't up to me. It never was. I can't make someone get saved. I can't even save my own soul let alone someone else's. Remember, "For by grace you have been saved through faith. And this is not your own doing; it is the gift of God, not a result of works, so that no one may boast." Ephesians 2:8-9

Truth #2

Your prodigal gets to choose. It's always been that way from the beginning of time, from the meal choice in the garden, to the march in the desert with Moses, to embracing the Messiah. A choice is set before your prodigal and only she/he can make it. Moses understood that perfectly in Deuteronomy 30:19, I call heaven and earth to witness against you today, that I have set before you life and death, the blessing and the curse. So choose life in order that you may live, you and your descendants."

Truth #3

You play a part in your prodigal's journey.
- ➢   You are thankful, "Oh give thanks to the Lord, call upon His name; Make known His deeds among the peoples." 1 Chronical 16:8.
- ➢   You call out evil and live righteously, "Therefore, since we have this ministry, as we received mercy, we do not lose heart, but we have renounced the things hidden because of shame, not walking in craftiness or adulterating the word of God, but by the manifestation of truth commending ourselves to every man's conscience in the sight of God." 2 Corinthians 4:1-2.
- ➢   You speak truth in love, "I have not hidden Your righteousness within my heart;
  I have spoken of Your faithfulness and Your salvation; I have not concealed Your lovingkindness and Your truth from the great congregation." Psalm 40:10

Truth #4

God promises to pursue your prodigal. When we feel like all is hopeless, it's not. There is someone in pursuit of your prodigal's heart that loves her/him more than you do. In Luke 19:10 it says, "For the Son of Man has come to seek and to save that which was lost." In Ezekiel 34:11, "For thus says the Lord God, "Behold, I Myself will search for My sheep and seek them out." And in Psalm 139 we learn there is no hiding from God, "Where can I go from Your Spirit? Or where can I flee from Your presence? If I ascend to heaven, You are there; If I make my bed in Sheol, behold, You are there."

I am comforted to know that the soul of my prodigal is in the hands of a loving God. He will do everything to save the prodigal, even die. And I can't help but be comforted by the God who is forever saving us. Jesus was hanging on a cruel cross when he had a soul next to him who made a lifetime of bad decisions. I suspect there were people in that man's life who questioned where his soul would soon reside. Then something happened. The man did inventory on his life and realized he deserved everything that was happening to him on that cross. He also realized the man next him did not. Reaching out in faith he made a request. "Jesus, remember me when You come in Your kingdom!" Luke 23:42. And that day a parent's prayer was answered, grace was granted, and a soul was saved.

Prayer

Dear Lord, thank you for loving and pursuing my prodigal. Thank you for never giving up. Holy Spirit please go where I cannot go, speak where I cannot speak, and fight against anything that keeps my prodigal from the cross. Amen

Light

"Behold, I stand at the door and knock; if anyone hears My voice and opens the door, I will come in to him and will dine with him, and he with Me" Revelations 3:20

Moving Forward

Don't make assumptions about salvation one way or the other. Instead, plan how to speak thankfulness, display righteousness, and lovingly share truth with your prodigal.

DAY TWENTY-THREE - WHEN OTHERS CRY

Truth Talk

It is hard enough when you yourself are grieving losses involving your prodigal. You get sad and then you try to move forward. But perhaps the most painful part of waiting for the prodigal is enduring the pain you see inflicted on those you love.

I become the mama bear, wanting to protect others from the wounds, but it's not easy to do. Sin is not practiced in isolation. Its effects leak into every area. It is at this realization that I catch myself and realize that I must practice restraint, even when it's hard. To retaliate, that's the flesh. To accuse, heap guilt, or even hurl threats against the prodigal is not helpful. My penchant for a pound of flesh will not achieve the righteousness God demands. He is seeking restitution and that looks different. It looks like Joseph.

In Genesis chapter 42, Joseph had risen to prominence as the leader of the land in Egypt, it was his duty to control grain distribution during a famine. Then one day he had visitors... his brothers. The ones who sold him into slavery, the ones who made his father cry believing his son was dead, the ones who allowed Joseph's mother to go to her grave believing she had lost a son, those brothers. There was no undoing the pain caused by their wickedness. Their prodigal behavior hurt many whom Joseph loved. Even though Joseph held great power, second only to

Pharaoh, yesterday's sorrows could not be undone, but the hope for the future was within his grasp. Joseph chose that. He stated, "As for you, you meant evil against me, *but* God meant it for good in order to bring about this present result, to preserve many people alive." Genesis 50:20.

Even when pain is part of your family's story, God is still at work in the lives of those affected by the prodigal. God can use difficult events, not just for our good, but for theirs as well. Sometimes that means removing the prodigal's influence. I've wondered what would have happened to Joseph if he stayed living with those prodigal brothers of his? Would they have worn him down to a point where he too would succumb to evil plans? Would he have learned forgiveness? Would he have grown in faith? Joseph isn't the only one. Before him, his father Jacob was separated from his twin Esau. It's difficult to know which was the prodigal, maybe both. But regardless, they were not good for each other and the separation worked God's plan for both of their lives.

Oftentimes, what we view as the sorrowful breaking down of family, is really God singling out the righteous for his purposes. I'm thankful that Abraham separated from his pagan family, and Ruth too. I'm glad that Jesus didn't let his prodigal half-brothers slow him down for God's redemptive plan. I'm richer because the apostle Paul chose faith in God's truth over Phariseetical family alliance.

On this side of eternity things are lost, relationships, time, and memories that will never be made. It's sad to us. But we serve a mighty God who creates beauty from ashes, using both tears and disappointment. The outcome is not always what we think, and rarely what we'd expect. We are asked to embrace the truth about our God who says,

"For My thoughts are not your thoughts, Nor are your ways My ways," declares the Lord. "For *as* the heavens are higher than the earth, So are My ways higher than your ways And My thoughts than your thoughts. "For as the rain and the snow come down from heaven, And do not return there without watering the earth And making it bear and sprout, And furnishing seed to the sower and bread to the eater; So will My word be which goes forth from My mouth; It will not return to Me empty, Without accomplishing what I desire, And without succeeding *in the matter* for which I sent it." Isaiah 55:8-11.

We are so limited in our ability to comprehend what God is doing. As Paul wrote in 1 Corinthians 13:12, "For now we see in a mirror dimly, but then face to face; now I know in part, but then I will know fully just as I also have been fully known." What looks like chaos is really a masterpiece in the making, and eternity changes everything. Just wait and see.

Prayer

Dear Lord, Your ways are not my ways. I avoid suffering and often times try to shield many from it, even when it is out of my power to do so. You are different; you are close to the brokenhearted, and save those who are crushed in spirit. I cannot change reality, but you are already using it for your good purposes. I will quiet myself and stand in awe of the one who is not thwarted by the actions of any man. You will use even brokenness to bless and to provide. Amen

Light

"Then I will make up to you for the years That the swarming locust has eaten, The creeping locust, the stripping locust and the gnawing locust, My great army which I sent among you. Joel 2:25

Moving Forward

Don't take sides regarding the prodigal. Rather pray for the person offended and wounded by the prodigal's behavior. Ask God to use this in her/his life for good and that bitterness will not take root.

DAY TWENTY-FOUR
- THE GRINCH

Truth Talk

Around Christmas time, many families enjoy watching holiday movies like: Home Alone, or Elf, or even the old traditional film, It's a Wonderful Life. But my favorites are still the cartoons: A Charlie Brown Christmas, Frosty the Snowman, Rudolph the Red Nosed Reindeer, and of course, The Grinch that Stole Christmas. The Grinch thought he had the perfect solution. He was tired of hearing the joyous praise of the citizens in Whoville from the town below. His plan was to highjack Christmas and steal all the things Mr. Grinch believed brought them the most joy: Ornaments and decorated trees, yummy food, and of course the presents. If those things were taken from their lives surely then the joyful celebration would forever cease. And while the Grinch story seems unique to us, it's been attempted before, long, long ago to a righteous man named Job.

According to the book that bears his name, Job was blameless, upright, fearing God and turning away from evil. Satan, however, had a plan. His goal was to humiliate God and insult the favor the Lord held upon Job. Satan's premise was that by stripping Job of his stuff (Grinch style) Job would no longer bow before his creator. So, with God's permission, Satan went to work. First, he hit his pocketbook by stripping away all his wealth in one day, and later, every one of his children were stricken dead. Job's response is shocking,

"Then Job arose and tore his robe and shaved his head, and he fell to the ground and worshiped. He said, "Naked I came from my mother's womb, And naked I shall return there. The Lord gave and the Lord has taken away. Blessed be the name of the Lord." Through all this Job did not sin nor did he blame God." Job 1:20-21.

Good on Job, but Satan wasn't finished. Before long, Job had lost his health, his reputation, and his relationship with his wife. And, despite shaky counsel, Job was able to come face to face with his God and proclaim, "Though he slay me, I will hope in Him." Job 13:15.

Today, we, like Job, have a far superior Grinch, one that won't repent and grow his heart, but will rather attempt to darken ours, to get us to refrain from praising and rejoicing the God he despises. But like the Who in Whoville, we have the blessing of extracting deep in our soul what really matters. 1 Corinthians 3:12-13 puts it this way, "Now if any man builds on the foundation with gold, silver, precious stones, wood, hay, straw, each man's work will become evident; for the day will show it because it is to be revealed with fire, and the fire itself will test the quality of each man's work."

Our response regarding the prodigal is an opportunity to see if our life is compliant with the fire code listed in scripture. When the fire of testing comes what is left standing? Without the testing we might never know until it's too late. In James 1:2-6, we are told, "Consider it all joy, my brethren, when you encounter various trials, knowing that the testing of your faith produces endurance. And let endurance have its perfect result,so that you may be perfect and complete, lacking in nothing. But if any of you lacks wisdom, let him ask of God, who gives to all generously and without reproach, and it will be given to him. But he must ask in faith without any doubting, for the one who doubts is like the surf of the sea, driven and tossed by the wind."

Ask yourself, do you possess endurance? How will you know if you have nothing to endure? Are you lacking in any area of your faith? How will you find out if your faith isn't tested? Are you in want of something? How do you know until you realize your need? Are you lacking wisdom? How will you find out until you are placed in a situation where your current resources fail?

My enemy is under the impression that attacking my family will work, that I will curse my God and die, but the Enemy is wrong. God, in all his wisdom, has used this trial to strengthen me and purify my faith. It's the kind of faith that can't be stolen away like tinsel on a tree. It's the kind of faith that will sing gloriously, and praise boldly the keeper of my soul. I identify with the Who's in Whoville who received a blessing that dreadful night. They lost everything at the hand of the Grinch, but when the sun rose on Christmas morning they still sang with joy. So can we.

Prayer

Dear Lord, I am thankful for your kindness, even in the mists of suffering. Thank you for your promise of eternal restoration. Allow me to thrive during the trials of life and use them to refine me as an equipped servant for your glory. Help me to sing out my gratitude regardless of my circumstances which are safely in your hand. Amen

Light

You have turned for me my mourning into dancing; You have loosed my sackcloth and girded me with gladness, That my soul may sing praise to You and not be silent. O Lord my God, I will give thanks to You forever. Psalm 30:11-12

Moving Forward

Go on a praise walk. As you stroll down the path sing songs to your Lord out loud. You will be surprised to find your spirit lifted high.

DAY TWENTY-FIVE
- RESCUING

Truth Talk

A prayer I would often pray as a parent was to keep anyone away from my children that prevented them from following Jesus, I just never dreamed that it might mean me. We parents love our prodigals, a lot. And when our prodigals get themselves into a jam, we are quick with solutions. Unfortunately, we can inject ourselves into circumstances where we stop being helpful and unintentionally become barriers to the cross. Our presence can stutter spiritual growth, leaving her/him dependent, clinging to us, not to God. Let me give you a true story visual that might help.

It was the summer of 1971 when I learned to swim. My mother took me to a club that offered city sponsored swimming lessons. As a little girl in the Dolphin swim class, I was treading along quite nicely until forced to face my greatest fear...the diving board. I'd like to tell you it was the high dive, so high that you'd get a nosebleed from the altitude change, but that would be a lie. Nevertheless, the platform was fierce, a virtual pirate's plank hovering over an ocean of water, threatening to cast me downward into Davy Jones' locker. My instructor was a seventeen-year-old boy, who no doubt signed up in hopes of earning enough money to take his girlfriend, Colleen, to the local Foster's Freeze on Main Street. In retrospect, he wasn't paid nearly enough.

"Come on, you can do it!" he coaxed from his catch point,

800 feet below the board, or so it seemed. Peering down I made a decision that day as firm as any Baptist convert coming forward on a Sunday night, I wasn't going to jump. Then the instructor did something outlandishly stupid, he got out of the pool and joined me on the board. "Let's jump together," he suggested. Yeah right. The minute he touched my shoulders I executed a defensive move so severe; it's been banned from legitimate self-defense classes across the world. Basically, I became a human octopus. Once he pried my arms from his neck, I locked my legs around his legs making it impossible for him to move without falling. Lifeguard boy was freaking out, after all it's not every day you have a third grader suctioned to your body.

Moms, previously spying on their precious tots in the floaters and sinkers class, were enthralled with the predicament this young boy had gotten himself into. I'm sure my mom was joining the others in their laugh-fest, making comments like, "I wonder who that child belongs to?" Eventually, my instructor realized there was only one way out. Yep, he jumped. And unlike the captain who goes down with the ship, I bailed from my human buoy and swam to the top. So, why did I abandon my human security blanket? Because when he stopped being there, I had to let go and trust in something else.

I'm reminded of the Bible verse that says, *"Trust in the Parent with all your heart and lean upon your Parent's understanding, and admit that they have all the solutions, and you won't suffer at all."* Oh wait, it doesn't say that. Rather, Proverbs 3:5-6 says it this way, "Trust in the Lord with all your heart, and do not lean on your own understanding. In all your ways acknowledge Him, and he will make your paths straight."

When I look upon scripture, I'm truly humbled at how many times there were no win scenarios where God showed up in big ways. It was God who gave elderly parents John the Baptist; God who provided mana from heaven to feed the children of Israel; God who took down the walls of Jerico; God who showed up in the burning furnace; God who through his Son, healed the lame and gave sight to the blind.

The lesson for me is this: continuing to rescue a needy person can suffocate me and exhaust my limited resources. Besides, I don't want to rob my prodigal of the opportunity to jump into a love that is always reliable, and deeper than the ocean itself, I want her/him to trust Jesus.

Prayer

Dear Lord, you are the safest place for the prodigal to land. Give me wisdom to know when to reach out and when to wait and pray. I will again pray that you remove anyone who gets in the way of your perfect plan for my prodigal, even if it's me. Amen

Light

The Lord's lovingkindnesses indeed never cease, For His compassions never fail. They are new every morning; Great is Your faithfulness. Lamentations 3:22-23

Moving Forward

Don't let bailing out your prodigal be your default. (It's difficult, I know). Rather, ask God whether you should intervene, if at all. Don't get in the way of God's plan to act in miraculous ways.

DAY TWENTY-SIX – THE RICH PRODIGAL

Truth Walk

Jesus had just finished blessing some children when approached by the man many bible scholars refer to as the rich young ruler. Mark 10:10-17, records it this way, "As He was setting out on a journey, a man ran up to Him and knelt before Him, and asked Him, "Good Teacher, what shall I do to inherit eternal life?" And Jesus said to him, "Why do you call Me good? No one is good except God alone. You know the commandments, 'Do not murder, Do not commit adultery, Do not steal, Do not bear false witness, Do not defraud, Honor your father and mother.'" And he said to Him, "Teacher, I have kept all these things from my youth up." Looking at him, Jesus felt a love for him and said to him, "One thing you lack: go and sell all you possess and give to the poor, and you will have treasure in heaven; and come, follow Me."

The man asked Jesus a very important question, "What shall I do to inherit eternal life?" Jesus answered him exactly according to the premise of earned salvation, the cost was complete and flawless obedience to the law. Jesus even highlighted a few of the commandments: don't murder, don't commit adultery, don't steal, don't lie, don't defraud, honor mother and father. As a side note, it's interesting that Jesus included "don't defraud" which isn't in the original Ten Commandment list (makes one wonder). Nevertheless, this man professed to be a keeper of them all. This man's grand profession of complete obedience needed some proof and Jesus asked for it, "One thing you lack: go and sell all you possess and give to the poor, and you will have treasure in heaven; and come, follow Me."

This grandiose idea that salvation was attainable reminded me of one of my husband's movie favorites, A Bridge Too Far. The story tells the true account of the 1944 military operation codenamed "Market Garden" from WWII. The mission was to secure various bridges in the Netherlands, particularly the Rhine River at Arnhem, to create a beachhead into German occupied enemy territory. The mission failed. With 17,000 allied troops killed. This led to many grasping for excuses: German fortification, miscommunication, or even lack of air support. The event was so influential in culture it prompted an idiom in the English language. "A bridge too far" has come to mean an unrealistic undertaking that exceeds the capabilities or resources of the person's attempt to achieve.

If we return to the rich young ruler, he too thought he could take enemy territory and overcome the chasm separating God and man, he too thought he had the proper resources to beat the odds and storm the gates of heaven, based upon his own goodness. He also was wrong. As a sinner he was incapable of settling the debt required to redeem his soul. His riches couldn't buy him heaven, and his lack of reliance on his greatest ally would prove detrimental to his goal of residency in heaven. After Jesus told him of his lack, and what would be required, the rich young ruler left, "But at these words he was saddened, and he went away grieving, for he was one who owned much property." His obedience and commitment to his mission had limitations.

Jesus commented upon the difficulty of those who have much wealth and how improbable it would be for them to be saved. "Again I say to you, it is easier for a camel to go through the eye of a needle, than for a rich man to enter the kingdom of God." The apostles were appalled, after all if a law-abiding Jew who most likely tithed a great deal couldn't earn a seat at the table, then who can? Jesus was quick to reveal the truth about salvation,

"Jesus replied, "The things that are impossible with people are possible with God." Luke 18:27) This entrance into eternal life has nothing to do with us, but everything to do with God's grace. It was too difficult for the rich young ruler. He thought by walking away he could keep the riches he had stored up. In reality, he lost everything.

So how does this relate to our prodigals? Sometimes God allows prodigals, or anyone else He loves for that matter, to lose everything in order to achieve the impossible. He calls them, and us, to follow.

Prayer

Dear Lord, I come without any resources that would make me acceptable to a Holy God. I cannot earn your great love, bestowed upon me by giving your Son to pay my debt. I give myself and everything I have to you for your glory, knowing that nothing lost on this side compares to the glory revealed in your eternal kingdom. I give you permission to use all of my resources on this side as you see fit, and I will gladly leave it all behind to follow and obey you. Amen

Light

For I consider that the sufferings of this present time are not worthy to be compared with the glory that is to be revealed to us. Romans 8:18

Moving Forward

Make a list of those in the Bible and what they gave up by following God. For example:

Moses
      Gave up: Safety Comfort
      Gained: Saving a nation, peace with God

Ruth
      Gave up: Her Culture
      Gained: A godly heritage

Matthew
      Gave up: Great Wealth
      Gained: Becoming a disciple of Jesus, a throne judging the tribes of Israel

Zacchaeus

Gave up: Money fraudulently earned
Gained: Salvation

DAY TWENTY-SEVEN - THE WORKERS

Truth Walk

I make bread. And by making bread I mean ordering wheat from a farm, shipping it to my home in air-tight gallon pails, milling it into flour, and then baking bread from scratch. Although very satisfying in taste and health benefits, making bread isn't as easy as it sounds. There must be the right measurement of flour (think grams not cups). The yeast must be live, as opposed to dead yeast (yeah that matters). The right amount of gluten needs to be developed, the rise just right, and over-risen bread is not the best. The internal bread temperature is important too.

Bread is often found in scripture. It's mentioned between 200 to 400 times depending upon your translation. Bread must be important, after all you don't see broccoli or potatoes mentioned that often. As early as Exodus we read about the children of Israel commanded to make unleavened bread (something I do by accident) before they fled Egypt. Later, God rained down bread from heaven, called manna, upon the ground for them to eat. In the book of 1 Kings, the prophet Elijah was fed bread by the birds of the air and later by a widow. In the book of Judges, bread was given to Gideon as proof that the Lord was in his presence. In the New Testament, it was out of Bethlehem, meaning House of Bread, that our Savior was born. And Jesus taught us to pray, "Give us this day our daily bread." And it was at Jesus' last supper that he broke the bread, proclaiming it to be his body given for us.

And in case we miss it, Jesus made the symbolism of bread perfectly clear in John 6:48-51, I am the bread of life. Your fathers ate the manna in the wilderness, and they died. This is the bread which comes down out of heaven, so that one may eat of it and not die. I am the living bread that came down out of heaven; if anyone eats of this bread, he will live forever; and the bread also which I will give for the life of the world is My flesh." Jesus is our bread of life.

Where do we fit in? Mark 4:26-29 explains, "The kingdom of God is like a man who casts seed upon the soil; and he goes to bed at night and gets up by day, and the seed sprouts and grows—how, he himself does not know. The soil produces crops by itself; first the blade, then the head, then the mature grain in the head. But when the crop permits, he immediately puts in the sickle, because the harvest has come."

I love this because it takes us through the entire process from seed sowing, to taking our hands off and going to bed where we wait in faith for those baby sprouts to develop; then overtime maturing until its ready for harvesting. But there's a problem. Jesus spoke of a dilemma when it came to harvesting wheat. In Matthew 9:37-38, we read, "Then He said to His disciples, "The harvest is plentiful, but the workers are few. Therefore beseech the Lord of the harvest to send out workers into His harvest."

Beloved, there are many souls out there just like our own precious prodigals that have made bad decisions, befriended the world and lost. But today they are hungry; they know their way didn't pan out as they thought, they are desperate, and they are ready for the harvest. And while your prodigal might still be dormant in the soil, or just a baby spout needing time, their prodigals are ready to hear about the bread of life who came down from heaven for them. I am praying for workers to cultivate the soil in my prodigal's life, how can I sit idle and not do the same for others who wait?

Prayer

Dear Lord, you are my Bread of Life, my daily nutrient, without you I cannot endure. The life you gave to me is rich, fresh and vital. I am yours and you are mine. Do not let me lose sight of the calling to make disciples, to share the gospel to a dying world. I will not hide your righteousness but speak of your love and faithfulness. There are prodigals out there who are now ready for harvest. You are the Lord of the harvest, direct me to the field that is ripe and ready to hear your truth and be saved.

Light

"Do you not say, 'There are yet four months, and then comes the harvest'? Behold, I say to you, lift up your eyes and look on the fields, that they are white for harvest. Already he who reaps is receiving wages and is gathering fruit for life eternal; so that he who sows and he who reaps may rejoice together." John 4:35-36

Moving Forward

Your prodigal may not yet be ready for harvest, do what the farmers do while waiting for their harvest to mature.

Farmers	Those who love the prodigal
Repair broken things that will be needed later	Make sure forgiveness on your part has been accomplished
Clear the field of pests	Remove things in our lives like bitterness, anger, malice
Continue to feed and exercise the animals	Make sure you are at your best physical and mental health

Prepare fields for the next planting season	Prepare for your next harvest that God is calling you to
Plan for rotations, purchases to be efficient	Invest in this current life stage for life efficiency

DAY TWENTY-EIGHT - THE RUN

Truth Walk

When we hear the famous story of the prodigal, as told by Jesus in the book of Luke, we often focus on the prodigal who messed up, and the other son, angry that a derelict like his brother could so easily get back into the good graces of dad. But for me, the real memorable character in this parable is the dad. Luke 15:20 says it this way, "So he (the prodigal) got up and came to his father. But while he was still a long way off, his father saw him and felt compassion for him, and ran and embraced him and kissed him."

As a mom who plays the part of the parent in this story, I am truly amazed at the father's reaction. What kind of dad is this that could quickly embrace a son who:

- Wished he were dead and took his money
- Violated all the religious teachings of his youth
- Spat on all the dad had done for him in the past
- Caused the father such anguish and pain as he mourned the loss of his son

Full of compassion? Embraced and kissed him? Really? It would have been more probable to have the father kick him in the rump and say, "About time you came to your senses, you got exactly what you deserved, welcome home, here's a shovel." But that's not at all the story Jesus told. Why?

To understand the message of the prodigal you have to read

the entire passage of Luke 15:1-32. In this chapter of the Bible Jesus is having a conversation with a bunch of prodigals, namely tax collectors and sinners. They were interested in what Jesus had to say. But also in this group were Pharisees and Scribes, the religious of the day. They were upset that Jesus was wasting his time on people they would call worthless. To set the stage on how God does business, Jesus told a few parables. The first is about a lost sheep, and how the shepherd was overjoyed to find it. The second story was about a woman losing a coin, and after searching was happy to find it. And finally, the prodigal story about a son who was morally lost and returned home. What do each have in common? The lamb was dumb for wandering away probably enticed by greener pastures or curiously; the woman was careless with her valuables; and the prodigal was ungrateful for leaving a good home in search of worldly lust and riches. But all were lost and now were found. At the end of each parable Jesus reveals who was lost and how God feels about it.

The Sheep   "I tell you that in the same way, there will be *more* joy in heaven over one sinner who repents than over ninety-nine righteous persons who need no repentance." Luke 15:7

The Lost Coin "In the same way, I tell you, there is joy in the presence of the angels of God over one sinner who repents." Luke 15:10

The Prodigal   "But we had to celebrate and rejoice, for this brother of yours was dead and *has begun* to live, and *was* lost and has been found.'" Luke 15:32

You see God is in the lost and found business: from a lost man and woman in the garden, to the Children of Israel, to the tax collectors and sinners sitting with Jesus, he goes out to find them and bring them home. God is all about the results. I'm so glad, because I don't want to be like the Pharisees and Scribes who didn't know they were lost, I know how lost I was until God saved me. God maintains that the lost have great value, and when they are found, well, that's something to celebrate. Our heavenly Father doesn't care much about the circumstances of what led to the lostness, only that his children are found.

My prodigal will come home someday, and I want my heart to be grateful to the good shepherd who loved enough to seek and even discipline her/him back to God. I want to ignore the events that carried the prodigal away. I just want to run.

Prayer

Dear Lord, please ready my heart to receive the prodigal, just as you received me. Thank you for your patience. None of us are worthy, yet you found me valuable enough to save me and put a coat of undeserved honor upon me and called me your own. Blessed be the grace of God. Help me extend it to others. Amen

Light

"Then the Lord passed by in front of him and proclaimed, "The Lord, the Lord God, compassionate and gracious, slow to anger, and abounding in lovingkindness and truth." Exodus 34:6

Moving Forward

Be prepared for the prodigal. That might mean making a welcome home sign, writing a love letter (or a book), or storing up a gift for that blessed day.

DAY TWENTY-NINE
- GOLDEN TICKET

Truth Walk

I remember going to my first walk-in movie. Growing up in California's Central Valley in the 60's there weren't a lot of theaters, only drive-ins. But on one rainy day my mom treated us to the thrill of a lifetime, an indoor movie theater! And because it was so memorable I will never forget the feature, the original Willy Wonka and the Chocolate Factory with Gene Wilder. In the movie the main character, Charlie was in pursuit of one of the five golden tickets, hidden in Wonka candy bars placed all over the world. Each ticket holder was granted entrance into the famous chocolate factory. Just like all the children in the theater, I dreamed of one day getting the "golden ticket."

But I'm not a child anymore. Today when I study my Bible, hoping to find scriptures that give me encouragement and hope while I wait for my prodigal to return, I want to make sure the theology is sound and not some childish golden ticket wish. This quest led me to study what is perhaps the most misinterpreted Bible verse. In Proverbs 22:6 we read, "Train up a child in the way he should go, Even when he is old he will not depart from it." Many well-meaning parents believe this verse guarantees salvation for their child. But does it?

The author for most of the book of Proverbs is Solomon, you know, the one who was raised by King David, the man after God's own heart. However, if you follow the life of Solomon, in 1 Kings 11:1-4 we see how the training in righteousness broke down, "Now King Solomon loved many foreign women along with the daughter of Pharaoh: Moabite, Ammonite, Edomite, Sidonian, and Hittite women, from the nations concerning which the Lord had said to the sons of Israel, "You shall not associate with them, nor shall they associate with you, for they will surely turn your heart away after their gods." Solomon had seven hundred wives, princesses, and three hundred concubines, and his wives turned his heart away. In 1 Kings 11:4 we read, "For when Solomon was old, his wives turned his heart away after other gods; and his heart was not wholly devoted to the Lord his God, as the heart of David his father *had* been."

Then there was Solomon's son Rehoboam, the beneficiary of the Proverbs who, according to 2 Chronicles 12, "did evil because he did not set his heart to seek the Lord." If being raised "in the way one should go" worked, you'd think an entire book read to Solomon's son should have done the trick. But that's not the case. Solomon failed miserably as a leader and a father, and his son was evil. If this verse isn't a guarantee of outcome for salvation what does this verse mean?

"Train up a child in the way he should go" does mean we are commanded to raise our children with truth and godly instruction. In Deuteronomy 6:7 we are admonished to do so, "You shall teach them diligently to your children, and shall talk of them when you sit in your house, and when you walk by the way, and when you lie down, and when you rise." That part is clear.

What does, "even when he is old he will not depart from it" mean. The Hebrew word for "depart" is translated, abolish or cut off. Biblical Counselor Pete Thompson interprets it this way, "When we teach young children we are creating a pathway in their brain for thinking. Most information will be processed and interpreted through this lens," he explains. "However, this in no way guarantees obedience. We often process information and still decide to do otherwise."

Perhaps, the most crucial truth about this verse is that it is not a guarantee of salvation, as many would hope. Raising a child is a "work", and we are saved by faith alone, not works, as written in Ephesians 2:8-9. The work isn't done by the child or the parent, it is work of God. To be honest, I'm one parent that is grateful that saving a soul isn't dependent upon my training abilities, but upon the finished work of Jesus Christ.

Prayer

Dear Lord, thank you for allowing me the privilege of teaching my child the word of God. I know it wasn't perfectly done. I'm so glad that my teaching proficiency, or lack of, isn't what saves my prodigal. Thank you that those embedded words are yours to use as you see fit. As David proclaimed, "My soul waits in silence, from him comes my salvation" and that includes my prodigal's soul too. Amen.

Light

For it is God who is at work in you, both to will and to work for *His* good pleasure.
  - Philippians 2:13

Moving Forward

Gold Promises:

- ☐ For the Son of man is come to save that which was lost. Matthew 18:11
- ☐ And hearing *this*, Jesus *said to them, "*It is* not those who are healthy who need a physician, but those who are sick; I did not come to call the righteous, but sinners." Mark 2:17
- ☐ "Fear not, for I am with you; be not dismayed, for I am your God; I will strengthen you, I will help you, I will uphold you with my righteous right hand." Isaiah 41:10
- ☐ For by grace you have been saved through faith; and that not of yourselves, *it is* the gift of God; not as a result of works, so that no one may boast. Ephesians 2:8-9.

DAY THIRTY - MOVING FORWARD

Truth Walk

I always used to say, "I love doing life with my family." The ins and outs the ups and downs and all the experiences that involves. For some, it can feel irresponsible to move on in life without your prodigal. We can all appreciate the "leave no man behind" mantra from the military. The Ranger code actually says, "I will never leave a fallen comrade to fall into the hands of the enemy." And the reality is, we are not 'leaving them behind.' The promise remains intact, "We will never leave them" since we pray for our prodigals daily. I bring him/her before the throne of our Father God and do battle in the heavenly realm for the restoration of his/her soul. I will never cease praying for him/her, ever. That said, I do have to move forward into my calling, the things God has for me to do. If my life stops at the door of grieving for my prodigal, then Satan has won, and the enemy will render the field of my life fruitless.

Moving Forward was the call given to one young pastor named Timothy. Timothy was very special to the apostle Paul. In Paul's first letter to Timothy, Paul refers to Timothy as "my true child in the faith." Biologically, Timothy had a Greek father and a Jewish mother, and we read in 2 Timothy 1, that it was his grandmother and mother that raised him in his faith. We don't know about Timothy's father, but it was evident that Paul took on the fatherly role of coaching this young man. Eventually, Timothy took on the leadership position for the church at Ephesus. Even then, Timothy thrived under Paul's instruction and encouragement, "Let no one look down on your youthfulness, but *rather* in speech, conduct, love, faith *and* purity, show yourself an example of those who believe," Paul encouraged in 1 Timothy 4:12.

But then things changed, due to Roman imprisonment and hardship, Paul wondered if he would ever again be with his beloved spiritual son. The letters written to Timothy from prison not only encouraged Timothy, but us today, as Paul gives clear direction in 1 Timothy 4:13-16 on how to move forward:

☐ Give attention to public reading of scripture
   (Stay in Church)

☐ Give attention to exhortation
   (find someone to encourage)

☐ Give attention to teaching
   (find someone to teach)

☐ Do not neglect your spiritual gifts
   (use your spiritual gift for God's glory)

☐ Be absorbed in them, so that your progress will be evident to all
   (your obedience and focus on God during trying times is a witness to others)

☐ Pay close attention to yourself and to your teaching
   (Don't worry about what others are doing wrong, focus on what you need to do right.)

☐ Persevere in all these things (a fancy word for don't give up, ever)

Moving forward always ushers in something new. And it often frightens us. We don't know how things will turn out. But what we don't realize is stagnation pays a price too. Abraham could have stayed on the farm, the second-generation Children of Israel could have remained in the desert, Jesus' disciples could have returned to fishing, and Timothy could have quit the pulpit after Paul was martyred. I'm so thankful they didn't. Likewise, how sad it would be when my prodigal arrives home, only to find me standing exactly where she/he left me.

Instead of craving my safe space, I need to see that something new is up ahead, realizing God is working in me, and the life of my prodigal; building in us eternal truths taught in ways I cannot even fathom. I'm going to do life with Jesus, running toward the prize, and someday we all will rejoice together for what God has done.

Prayer

Dear Lord, I call out to you for boldness to go forward. I bring with me the prayers of my loved ones and am expectant on what you can and will do. Allow me to move into fruitful labor. I am excited to see what you've planned. You are writing a story of love and redemption in my very own family and I want to be faithful to see it through to your completion. Amen

Light

"Do not call to mind the former things or ponder things of the past. "Behold, I will do something new, now it will spring forth; will you not be aware of it? I will even make a roadway in the wilderness, Rivers in the desert. Isaiah 43:18-19

Moving Forward

God is calling you to move forward. Walking boldly into new opportunities where He is calling you. He has uniquely gifted you for this next season of your life. Take it on and watch his glorious story unfold.

CONCLUSION

I loved going to Grandma's house. Her home was super clean, you could eat off her kitchen floor. We loved music. She had one of those old record player consoles filled with classic albums, and together we'd listen to Andy Williams and Elvis. Bing Crosby was one of her favorites, and I always think about her when I hear White Christmas played during the holiday season. I miss her. It's the little things. Sometimes I can smell her Jergens lotion. I reminisce about the times she took me out to lunch at the chicken pie café down the block from her house. I enjoyed playing in her tiny backyard and eating watermelon on the patio. "Don't spit the seeds in my flowerbed," she would call out, "I don't want melons in my daffodil garden." Good memories.

My grandma was a prodigal. At the tender age of 16 she ran off with my much older grandfather whom she met a few months earlier at a military officer's dance in Casa Grande, Arizona. Her parents were heartbroken. I have a memoir passed down to me from my father who recounts her parents' disappointment. Her mother, my great-grandmother, made them promise to get married in a church. And so it goes.

God loves prodigals, if he didn't none of us would be here. We have all, at one time or another, walked away from our one true love. It happened right away in the garden, when Adam and Eve chose to disobey. Not too long after that we see Noah and his family becoming last survivors in a world of prodigals who turned from God. Moses struggled with an entire nation of prodigals and lost his temper more than once. Even King David, beloved of God, lost his way for a time. Let's face it, the human race is full of prodigals.

But again, God loves prodigals, so he had a plan. He sent

his only Son (not a prodigal) to receive all the punishment that every prodigal deserved. Redemption at the cross was a way to buy prodigals back from perdition. God laid down a blood-stained road, paving the way for the prodigal's return. That road still exists. It's there for those who choose to repent, acknowledging their lack and need for a Savior.

I remember when my grandma passed away. In those days I was a busy young working girl with things to do and people to see, but I knew I wanted to visit before she was gone. Grandma had never been against God, I knew she believed God existed, but had never heard her pray, and for sure knew she hadn't been in church for a very long time. I hoped that she was saved. At the foot of her bed, I asked her if she loved Jesus and wanted to go to heaven. Through the noise of the oxygen machine, she answered me, "Jesus said that he goes and prepares a place for us. I believe him." And later that week another prodigal went home.

CLOSING PRAYER

"Thy will be done." It was the last recorded prayer Jesus prayed before his crucifixion. The Father requested something from Jesus, grieving his very soul. An innocent man was asked to carry the punishment for a sinful world. Jesus asked if there could be another way, but in the end, he was asked to drink the cup, to set sinners free. On this side of eternity, we don't always get what we imagined. And we have the right to ask if there is another way when things go bad, but when the Amen comes, it must be with submission to God. The process of saving a soul looks messy, often there must be suffering. Still, we don't suffer in vain, there is a cross and an empty tomb, we have hope, we have peace.

Dear Lord, none of my sorrows have caught you by surprise. Just as you predicted the cross so many prophets ago, you predicted your resurrection, and the joy set before us. While we wait for your glorious plan to be revealed, let me be fruitful and make the most of my good works, predestined before time began. When I rise each morning let me follow Jesus' example proclaiming, "Thy will be done."

Amen

RESOURCES

https://www.petethompson.org/

https://www.focusonthefamily.com/christian-counselors-network/

PRAYER TO ACCEPT JESUS

If you have never asked the Savior, Christ Jesus, into your life, today can be your day to receive God's greatest gift.

Dear God,

I have sinned against you and against others, and I could never be good enough to enter Your Kingdom. Please forgive me. Thank you for sending Your Son, Jesus, to die on the cross for my sins, and to pay my way into heaven. I now give my life over to You as a living sacrifice. I want to do things Your way. Come into me, Holy Spirit, and direct my path in the way everlasting. Amen.

OTHER WORKS BY LYNNE THOMPSON

Thompson, Lynne & Pete Thompson, LCSW, 2025, Tools for Better Communication.

Thompson, Lynne & Pete Thompson, LCSW, 2017, How Anxiety Destroyed King Saul.

Thompson, Lynne, 2017, Wag the Mouth: Series Book 1.

Thompson, Lynne, 2017, Wag the Teacher: Series Book 2.

Thompson, Lynne, 2008 The Official Soccer Mom Devotional, Regal Publishing.

Thompson, Lynne, Breaking up with Bad Company, Bible.org

Contact the Author at: Lynne@LynneThompson.net   or

https://www.petethompson.org/

BOOKS FOR PURPOSEFUL LIVING TODAY

Visit: https://petethompson.org/shop/

Tools for Better Communication
Pete & Lynne Thompson introduce five communication tools that will bring peace and healing to your relationship. It's not too late to honor God with the way you speak to the people you care about.

How Anxiety Destroyed King Saul
Pete and Lynne Thompson invite you to sit-in on three counseling sessions featuring a biblical character who needed healing from this very condition. With over 35 years in the mental health field, Pete offers biblical insight for this challenging, yet treatable mental health issue.

Wag The Mouth
Can geeks become the most popular people on campus? They can if Tori Sanchez is in charge! Tori has a plan for creating a 'geek-friendly' school, but it's going to take a cow, some risk, and maybe just a little romance. It's time for the rise of the Geek Elite!

Wag The Teacher

Can the coolest teacher on campus be transformed into a geek? Tori is back again, and this time tries her hand at matchmaking. Her plan includes a crazy makeover for one single mom, and geek school for one lucky teacher.

ABOUT THE AUTHOR

God is not done with your prodigal, or you!

Somewhere during our livin' the dream lifestyle, a child was lost. Not by death, although at times it feels like it, but in a dark forest of rebellion. At some point during the 'growing up loved' and 'learning to leave the nest' my child took the wide road; the one that led away from our family and all that we valued. I know I'm not alone. There are thousands of parents and family members just like me who are in shock, asking over and over again,

"What happened?"

In her book, Lynne Thompson offers a devotional filled with inspirational stories on how to keep our eyes on what's important, as we walk this holy journey, waiting for our prodigals to come home. Each day offers a biblically focused story, a prayer, a biblical verse for encouragement, and an activity to help you move forward during this trial.
Hope is waiting.

Lynne Thompson is an author, speaker, radio personality, Bible teacher, wife, and mother. For years she was the voice offering 'Soccer Mom Moments' for Focus on the Family's Weekend Magazine, broadcasting throughout the United States and Canada, to over one million listeners. She is author of several books including: The Official Soccer Mom Devotional (Regal Books), The Wag Series (teen market), and How Anxiety Destroyed King Saul and How to Fight Fair and Win: Tools for Communication (co-authored with husband Pete Thompson, LCSW). Lynne's favorite role is wife to Pete of 38 years and mother to their two adult children. They reside in Texas.

ISBN 979-8-218-65667-6

9 798218 656676

Made in the USA
Coppell, TX
10 August 2025

53038219R10079